N.E.W & REVISED edition

STICK IT!

99 D.I.Y. DUCT TAPE PROJECTS

by T.L. BONADDIO

Illustrated by ANDREW TOMLINSON

RUNNING PRESS
PHILADELPHIA • LONDON

Published by Running Press,
A Member of the Perseus Books Group

Printed in China

Books published by Running Press are available at special dis-
counts for bulk purchases in the United States by corporations,
institutions, and other organizations. For more information,
please contact the Special Markets Department at the Perseus
Books Group, 2300 Chestnut Street, Suite 200, Philadelphia, PA
19103, or call (800) 810-4145, ext. 5000, or e-mail special.mar-
kets@perseusbooks.com.

ISBN 978-0-7624-4753-4

Library of Congress Control Number: 2012935961
E-book ISBN 978-0-7624-4298-0

9   8   7   6   5   4   3   2   1
Digit on the right indicates the number of this printing

Cover and interior design by Ryan Hayes
Illustrations by Andrew Tomlinson and T.L. Bonaddio
Photographs by Ryan Hayes and Jonathan Weed
Photo and style for "Striper" table by Eric Puglisi & Adam Slevin
Edited by Kelli Chipponeri
Typography: Clarendon & Din Schrift

Running Press Book Publishers
2300 Chestnut Street
Philadelphia, PA 19103-4371

Visit us on the web!
www.runningpress.com

CONTENTS

The

DT (DUCT TAPE)

CRAFTSTER'S

Manifesto

Duct Tape can change your life in so many ways. No doubt, it probably already has. Some for good, like keeping your broken refrigerator door handle on for the millions of trips you make to it for munchies. And some for . . . well . . . not so good, like being DTed to the flag pole outside of school because someone felt you'd be missing out on life without that humiliation.

This book is not meant to enhance or encourage those types of life-changing experiences, but by all means don't let me stop your bad self from experimenting. After all, it's fun, courageous curiosity that will fuel your creative drive through the projects here.

From wicked wallets that will make your boyfriend/girlfriend/mom/barista jealous, to punked out paper goods, you can rile up your world with all of that, wild wearables, and more. Just flip these pages, stock up on colorful rolls of DT (and other tapes, as well!), and tune in to your imagination. Let your rockin' self unroll.

WARNING:
STICKY STUFF!

To state the obvious—DT is some pretty sticky stuff. Such as when you get "stuck" in life and want to bash your head onto hard surfaces, there are going to be frustrating times working with this oh-so-durable medium. Please don't intentionally harm yourself. If pieces of tape get tangled and mangled—and they will, trust me—simply rip yourself a new piece. Start over. And if worse comes to worse, put the DT down and step away from the project. Breathe deep—don't verbally or physically bash anyone or anything in your way—and return when you've chilled.

Just remember that you are brilliant no matter what your pretentious craftster friends say. And if you're a pretentious craftster, well, you already know you're the shizz, so go on!

PROJECT DIFFICULTY LEVELS:

**** *Dude, my five-year-old sister could do that.*

**** *Who says you can't chew gum, talk, and cut tape at the same time?*

**** *Take a lesson from mama: listen, sit your butt down, and be patient.*

**** *Don't even think about operating heavy machinery.*

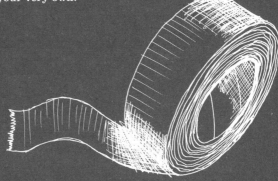

BEFORE YOU
ROCK&UNROLL

So you're psyched up on caffeine, and visions of DT wallets—and how much dough you can roll in from them—dance in your head. Now where do you go? Before you race to unroll, my friends, we need to make a few pit-stops down the T3 trail, to get the lowdown on necessities: Tools, Tips, and Techniques. By the end, your brain will be busting with the know-how to get through any project here—and on your way to becoming the DT masters of your very own.

TOOLS

Think of dealing with DT as paper or fabric and not your dad's emergency plumbing repair kit. Here is a list of tools that will come in handy for almost every project. Any other tool that's project-specific will be listed on the project page.

- Ruler
- Scissors
- Craft knife
- Cutting mat
- Permanent fine-tip marker

UNLOCK THE LINGO

SSD = sticky-side down

SSU = sticky-side up

SSS = sticky-side suck-face (2 pieces of DT making out, sticky side to sticky side)

E2E = edge to edge

H-axis = horizontal axis

V-axis = vertical axis

LFT = left

RT = right

LSB = long side (on the) bottom

SSB = short side (on the) bottom

Warp = in the process of weaving, a set of DT strips that run lengthwise

Weft = in the process of weaving, DT strips that run crosswise

TIPS

WHERE DO YOU FIND ALL THE AWESOME COLORED DT AND OTHER NEAT-O TAPES?

Become a scavenger for myriad tape varieties that exist and where you can find them. Common places that carry them: arts & craft supply stores, home improvement stores, and general stores. Oh yeah, and that thing called The Internet.

WHERE'S THE BEST PLACE TO STICK IT?

Work on a hard, smooth surface, onto which DT can easily be stuck and removed.

To be efficient, at times you'll want to cut many strips of DT before using them. Set aside space for these (i.e. edge of table/desk, not your dog). Which brings me to . . .

WHEN YOU SAY "WRAP TAPE AROUND" YOU MEAN STICKY SIDE DOWN, RIGHT?

Click on your common sense. You're wicked smart. I promise not to DT you to a pole, but don't make me talk to you like I'm teaching grandma to scrapbook.

HOW DO I MEASURE 3-D THINGS, LIKE MY WRIST OR RING-FINGER, FOR PROJECTS?

Use a piece of paper or string, that way you can wrap, mark, and transfer measurements to your DT.

TECHNIQUES

HOW TO MAKE A SHEET OF DT FABRIC

This is the core of almost every project—learn it, love it, use it.

1. Side A: start with 1 DT strip SSU. Then SSS another strip about ¼" from the top (unless otherwise instructed). Fold that top ¼" over to seal the edge.

Tip: Ignore initial precision and overshoot the measurements of your strips. At the end, trim down the fabric with exactitude.

2. Flip the sheet over to side B. Add another strip of DT SSD, so it overlaps the sticky tab.

3. Continue to add strips to the sticky tabs, flipping between Side A and Side B, until you've reached the approximate sheet size the project calls for. Then fold over the edge of the last strip to seal.

4. With a straight edge and craft knife, trim your DT sheet to precision.

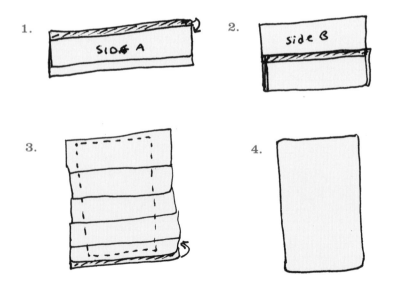

1.   SIDE A

2.   side B

3.

4.

This is a great decorating technique—pimp out your projects with a personal touch.

MATERIALS

- Tracing paper
- Photo/image
- Soft-lead pencil
- Hard-lead pencil

1. Place tracing paper on top of image. Use a pen to outline the image.

2. Remove the tracing paper and flip it over. Retrace the outline with a soft-lead pencil.

3. Flip over the tracing paper again so it reads right. Place it on top of the DT and retrace the lines with a hard-lead pencil.

4. Remove tracing paper. The lines on the DT may be faint, but strong enough to see where you should cut with a craft knife.

5. Peal away the DT around the image and the silhouette remains.

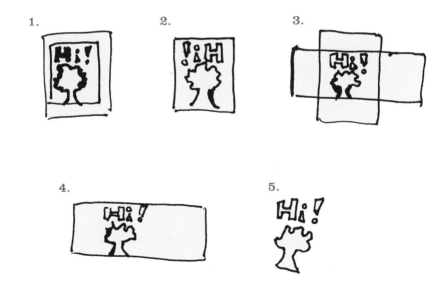

1.

2.

3.

4.

5.

CHAPTER ONE

WALLETS

1.0 ✳✳✳✳
LIP-LOCK

To David and Delilah, money talks loudly. They keep it mum within these Duct Tape walls, until they want to let it loose.

MATERIALS

- DT (red)
- Clear packing tape
- Double-stick tape
- Deco fastener
- String

1.0 Create one 8½" x 11" sheet—the long side on the bottom.

2.0 Fold the LFT and RT sides to the middle and crease their edges. Unfold.

3.0 Fold top to bottom, E2E, along the H-axis. Unfold. (You should see six panels. Think of them as #1-6, clockwise.)

4.0 Section 1 (ID holder):
(a.) Cut out one 2¼" x 3½" window.
(b.) Cover the whole front and back with clear tape.

5.0 Section 2 (card holder):
With a 1" margin on each side, slice across the H-axis. At each end of that cut, make one 2" vertical cut.

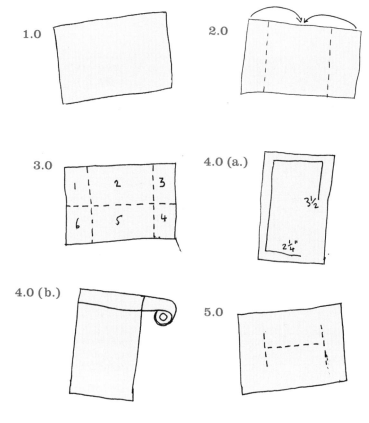

1.0

2.0

3.0

4.0 (a.)

4.0 (b.)

5.0

Section 4 (closure):
Attach deco fastener 1" from the RT vertical edge, in the middle.
Knot one 6" strand of string to the fastener.

Section 6 (closure):
Attach deco fastener 1" from the LFT vertical edge, in the middle.

Turn the whole sheet over to the other side. Attach double-stick tape to the perimeter of section 2. Then fold the bottom edge of the whole sheet to the top edge. Apply pressure over section 2.

Flip over again, so you're viewing the wallet interior. Seal the following edges with ½" thick DT strips: LFT vertical side of section 1 and across the top of section 3.

Fold in the LFT and RT flaps to the center and wrap the string around the opposite deco fastener to keep wallet closed.

6.0

7.0

8.0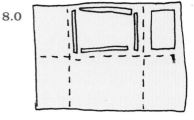

9.0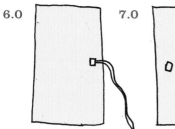

10.0

NOTES:

1.1 ✳✳✳✳
WANNABE

Like Harvey, some wallets never learn to grow up. Some wallets just pretend. And some wallets survive like this in the "real world" just fine.

MATERIALS

- DT (gray)
- Clear packing tape
- Gaffers tape (1" white)

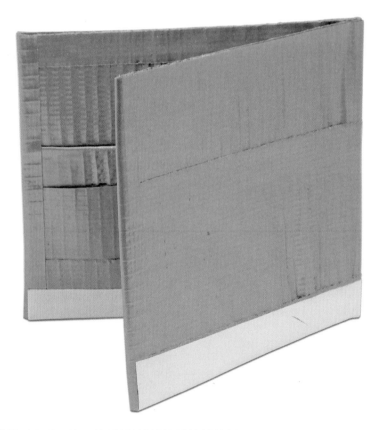

1.0 For wallet base: Create one 8" x 8" sheet.

1.1 Fold it approximately in half. (The fold should fall naturally along the crease of a strip of DT.) Trim excess, to create a 3½" height.

2.0 For credit card pockets: create one 3¾" x 4" sheet.

2.1 Fold along the natural H-axis, which should result with about a ¼" margin at the top.

3.0 For plastic ID sleeve: create one 5¼" x 4" sheet with clear tape.

3.1 Fold along the natural H-axis, measuring against your ID. Keep a small margin on the top of the back sleeve.

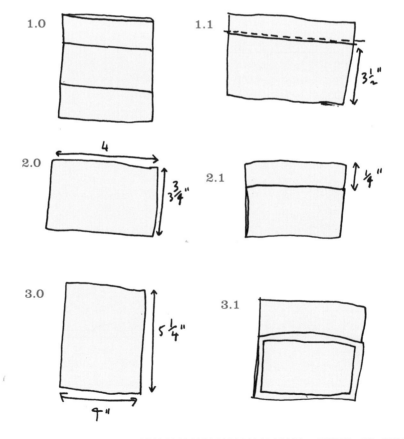

To attach the credit-card pocket and ID sleeve to the wallet:

Cut:
(a.) One 1" x 4" DT strip
(b.) Two ½" x 3½" DT strips
(c.) One 3½" x ¾" DT strip
(d.) One 8" Gaffers tape strip

With the wallet base fold on the bottom, place the credit card pockets on the LFT and ID sleeve on the RT, aligning both with the bottom.

Attach tapes accordingly:
(a.) Horizontally over excess margin of ID sleeve.
    Align with top edge.
(b.) Wrap vertically around the LFT and RT edges to seal.
(c.) Vertically along the middle.
(d.) Wrap horizontally around the bottom fold.

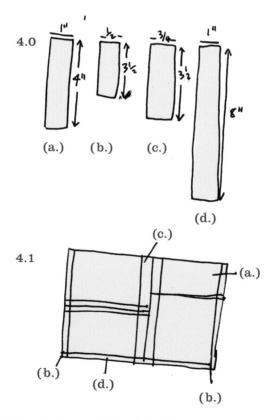

NOTES:

1.2 ✳✳✳✳
TWIST

Pop a quarter into the jukebox, order a milkshake, and tell Danny to put his frickin' wallet away because you've got it handled.

MATERIALS

- DT (black, pink, white)
- 2 circle-shaped magnets

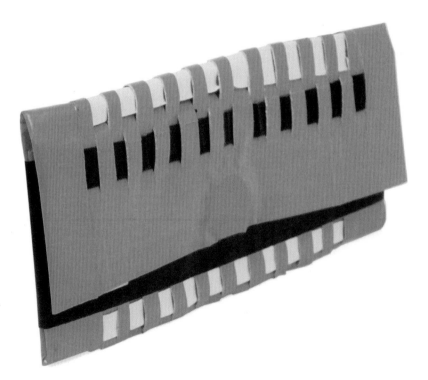

1.0 Create one 9" x 6½" pink sheet. On the first SSU strip place 1 magnet in the middle and proceed as usual.

2.0 Fold the bottom of the sheet up, so it creates a pocket about 2½" high. Fold the top down over it and estimate placement of the second magnet.

Tip: Folds will occur naturally—work with them, not against them.

2.1 Hold the magnet in place and unfold. Then place one 6½" pink strip SSD over it.

3.0 Create warp: Keep ¾" margins on the LFT and RT sides and use the magnets as margin points for the top and bottom. Slice vertically every ¼" within those margins.

4.0 Create white and black weft: Cut two 6½" strips of each color. Work with one strip at a time SSU, with the SSB. SSS the LFT and RT sides to the middle.

4.1 Cut down the V-axis.

1.0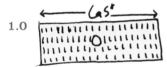

2.0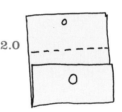

2.1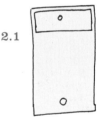

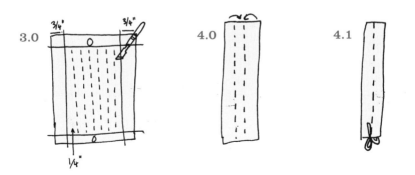

5.0

To weave: Begin with the black weft and bring it up from the bottom of Slit 1. Then push it down through Slit 2. Repeat that pattern until it reaches the end. With the white weft, push it through the top of Slit 1 and pull it up through Slit 2. Repeat the pattern until the weave is complete.

6.0

Cut two 9" strips of pink DT and SSD line up ¾" along the LFT over the loose weft and wrap around to cover the other side's weft. Repeat on the RT side.

7.0

Fold the bottom of the fabric up, to create bill pocket. Cut one 8¼" strip of black DT. Wrap it around the front of the pocket and around the edges to the front of the wallet. When you close the wallet you should be able to see the black tape a bit.

5.0

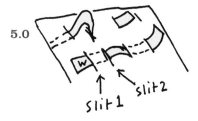

6.0

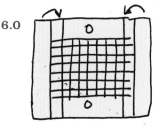

7.0

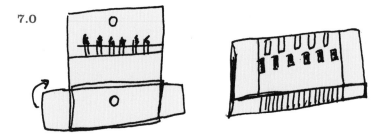

NOTES:

1.3 ✳✳✳✳
DIRTY

Lesley liked putting his money where his mouth was. Eww. He should plant his dough here and dig it out whenever he wants instead.

- DT (brown, grass-green, lime-green)

1.0 Create 1 sheet of fabric about 7" x 10".

2.0 LSB, fold it approximately in half and trim to 9¾" x 3¼".

3.0 Unfold and cut along the H-axis to the ⅓ point from the LFT, then ⅓ from the RT.

4.0 Fold RT flaps over the middle to the ⅓ point. Then fold the LFT flaps over the RT ones to the ⅔ point.

5.0 Lift up the middle, so the center fold peaks like a mountain and press sides together.

6.0 Tip the wallet to the LFT and let the front and back flaps fall to your tabletop to form an upside down "T." With one ½" x 3½" strip of brown DT seal the bottom part of the wallet (the seam of the "T") by wrapping it around it, and the middle spine of the wallet (the bottom stem of the "T").

7.0 When you hold the wallet upright again, you should have 2 pockets on the inside with a front and back flap falling over them. You will also have a third pocket between the 2 left-hand spines.

*Decorate flaps with other tapes as desired.
For my design, see pg. 243, steps 4.0-4.1.*

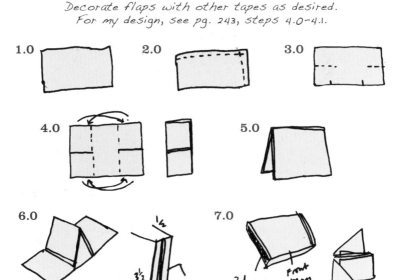

1.4 ✳✳✳✳
LUCKY

Savanna's mom used to tell her how lucky heads-up pennies were. But Savanna liked to think all circles were lucky. And so she made this wallet to carry it with her wherever she went.

MATERIALS

- DT (gray, red, black, white)

See pp. 19-20, steps 1.0-4.1 ["Wannabe"]

Open the wallet to view the outside. Cut out various sized red, black, and white DT circles and adhere them to the outside of the wallet.

2.0

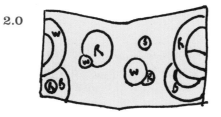

NOTES:

1.5 ✳✳✳✳
QUEEN

There's a party on the dance floor and the world's her stage. No queen has pockets. They're like Karen, who won't dare wave her hands like she doesn't care.

MATERIALS
- DT (purple, black)
- Gaffers tape (1" gray)
- Electric tape (black)
- 2 Heavy duty snaps (5/8")
- Magnetic purse clasp

TOOLS
- Jumbo snap fastener tool kit

FOR WALLET ENCLOSURE:

1.0 Create one 4" x 5½" purple sheet. With the SSB, fold the bottom towards the center to make a "wallet-shape" (about ¼ below the wallet flap fold).

2.0 Cut two 2" x ½" purple strips and wrap each one around the LFT and RT edge to seal the sides.

3.0 Attach Gaffers tape along the bottom of the wallet, front and back. Do the same with black electric tape, but leave a little gray tape showing below it.

4.0 Attach magnetic purse snaps.

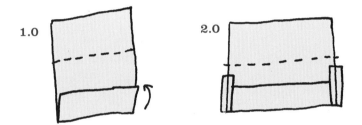

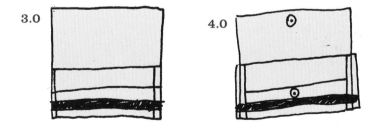

FOR WRIST-WRAP BAND:

1.0	Measure your wrist 1¾" up from your hand and add 1".
2.0	Create 1 black DT sheet based on that measurement.
3.0	Make slices across the bottom and top flap fold of the wallet. The slice length = the thickness of your wristband.
3.1	Slide wristband into the top, through the inside of the wallet and out of the bottom.
4.0	Attach snaps to the wristband.

1.0-2.0 See p. 59 steps 1.0-2.0, ["Black"]

3.1

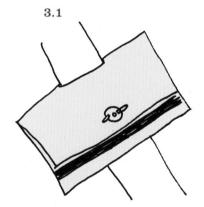

4.0

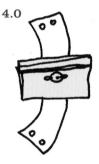

NOTES:

....

....

....

....

....

....

....

NOTES:

✳✳✳✳

SPINNER

Adam owes you ten bucks because he had to pay Sue who owed it to Lou who owed it to Frank who owed it to you . . . for making him this wallet.

MATERIALS

- DT (orange, grass-green, black)
- Square deco fasteners

TOOLS

- Hole punch (⅛")

1.0 Create six 3" x 4½" DT sheets (2 green, 2 orange, 2 black).

2.0 Cut one 3" strip of each color and cut in half longwise. Then cut one 4½" strip of each color.

3.0 Take the 2 black sheets and fold Sheet 2 from the bottom to about ¼ the distance from the top (follow the natural crease of the DT). Then place that piece on top of Sheet 1 and tape the 2 together by folding the smaller DT strips around the edges of the sides that are equal in length. Repeat this entire step with the green and orange sheets.

4.0 Take each card holder individually and punch a hole in the upper LFT corner.

Note: Whichever color you choose as your "front piece," turn it over so the card pockets do not show, then punch a hole in the upper LFT corner.

Then stack them so the holes line up and attach the deco fastener.

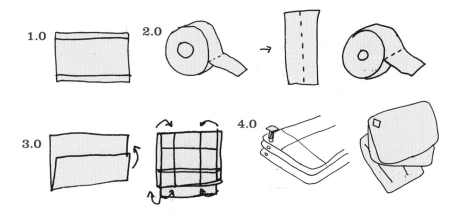

NOTES:

UNDERGROUND

Maura's friends hear it. Her mom hears it. Her postman hears it. Her postman's dad hears it. It may be London calling. But I bet you it's money.

MATERIALS

- DT (dark blue)
- Clear packing tape
- Adhesive Velcro
- Map of the London Underground

FOR FRONT FLAP (LONDON UNDERGROUND MAP):

Buy a paper L.U. Map (or print one off the Web). The maximum size it should be is 5" x 7" (LSB), the minimum 4" x 6½". "Laminate" the front with clear tape and cover the back with blue DT.

Create 1 sheet of blue DT:
- 2 x the height of your map + the same width across.
- Flip your L.U. Map upside down (face down) and, between the first 2 strips of the DT sheet, sandwich ½" the bottom edge.

To make the bill holder, fold the bottom edge up to a little less than the ⅓ point from the bottom.

FOR 2 SETS OF CREDIT CARD HOLDERS:

The height of the pocket of your bill holder = the width of the credit card holder. Cut 3 strips of DT to that measurement and create 1 DT sheet. Repeat the process 3 more times, for a total of 4 components.

Keep 2 sheets flat. For each of the other 2, fold along the natural H-axis, which should result with about one ¼" x ½" margin at the top.

Individually align each on top of a flat sheet, with the bottom edges. One will be Set 1, the other Set 2.

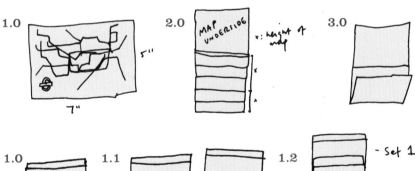

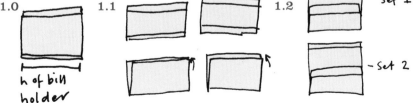

Take the large wallet sheet and place Set 1 and Set 2 on the exterior flap of the bill holder. Align the outer edges, and the opening of the pockets should face towards the middle.

Cut:
- 2 DT strips (height of the bill holder)
- 2 DT strips (width of the bill holders)

To seal the bill holder and credit card holder into place, wrap these strips around the edges in this order: top, LFT, RT, then bottom.

Decorative option:
Using 2" strips of Artist tape (red, baby blue, and yellow), wrap the LFT and RT bill holder edges.

For a secure closure, open your wallet and adhere Velcro to the center top and bottom.

2.0

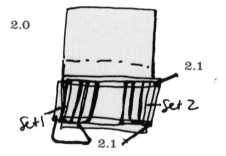

2.1

Set 1

Set 2

2.1

3.0

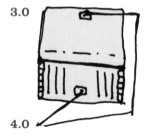

4.0

NOTES:

CHAPTER TWO
WRIST WEARABLES

2.0 ✱✱✱✱
FORTUNATE

Sia gets a message every time she orders takeout—which she admits, she does often. Ah, yes, good fortune! This one's a keeper.

MATERIALS
- DT (grass-green, yellow)
- Clear packing tape
- Fortune cookie fortune
- Double-stick tape

TOOLS
- Star-shaped hole punch

1.0 Measure your wrist 1¾" up from your hand and add 2".

2.0 Create 1 green DT sheet with 2 strips based on that measurement.

2.1 Cut two 3½" strips of yellow and set aside.

3.0 Cut 1 piece of double-stick tape to the length of your fortune and adhere to the back of it. Center it and stick it on the green band.

4.0 SSU and SSB, fold 1 of the yellow DT strips to the ¾ point. Repeat with the second yellow piece.

4.1 Hole punch 3 stars on the non-sticky side along the middle on each strip.

1.0
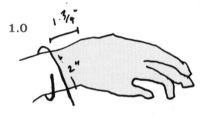

2.

2.1
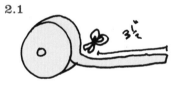

3.0
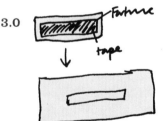

4.0

4.1

SSD, place 1 strip on each side of the fortune and wrap the ends around the band.

"Laminate" the whole band with clear tape.

Trim edges and create waffle weave clasp by following the cutting marks in the diagram.

Slip the center strand through the inner loop you create and tuck the 2 outer pieces underneath the slices on the edge.

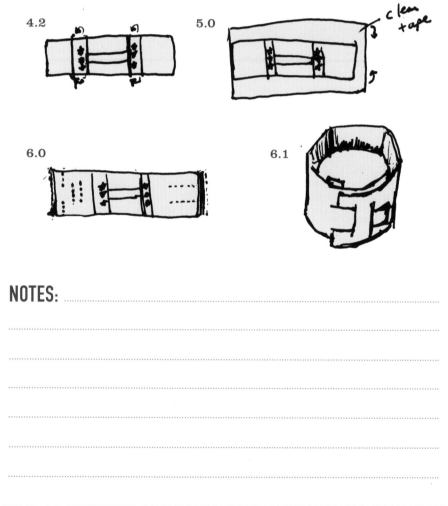

4.2

5.0

clear tape

6.0

6.1

NOTES:

NOTES:

IMAGINER

What if you lived in seclusion, like Evan, where the closest company is a bird you call Bird? Scratch that. Cuff this people-pleaser on yourself instead and you'll never be alone.

MATERIALS
- DT (white, black)
- 2 Heavy duty snaps (5/8")

TOOLS
- Jumbo snap fastener tool kit

1.0 Measure your wrist 2½" up from your hand and add 1".

2.0 Create 1 white sheet with 3 strips based on that measurement.

3.0 Create black DT silhouettes of people [see page 13] and adhere to the top of the white band.

4.0 Apply snaps at each end.

1.0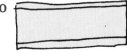

2.0

3.0

4.0

NOTES:

RHAPSODIC

Piper's mom says, "You're as musical as Billy Joel . . . the mechanic." It doesn't matter—she wanders to her own tune with this wrist-wrap.

- DT (black, white)

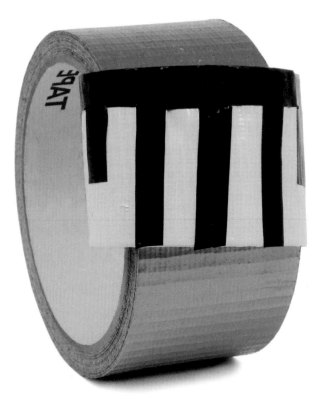

Measure your wrist 1¾" up from your hand and add 2".

Create 1 white sheet with 2 strips based on that measurement. Then cut 1 black strip to that measurement.

With the black strip (LSB), cut vertical "fringe" starting ½" from the top. Then make horizontal slices at the ½" point between every other vertical cut. Your cuts should create rectangles, which you can trash. The remaining piece is your "keyboard."

Stick the keyboard on top of the white fabric, lining up the top edge. Then trim the edges of your keys.

Create waffle weave clasp by following the cutting marks in the diagram.

Slip the center strand through the inner loop you create and tuck the 2 outer pieces underneath the slices on the edge.

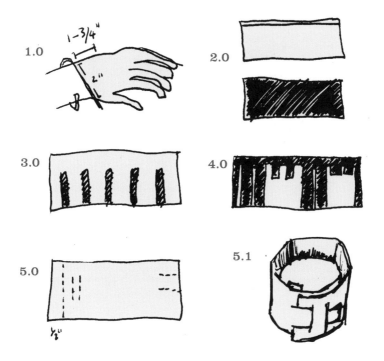

LOCO-MOTIVE

Soft lights. Stargazing. Snuggling (and snoring) next to your love.
Capture all the moments, like Liza, that make your heart go chug-a-choo
in this wrap-a-roo.

MATERIALS
- DT (dark blue, white)
- Electric tape (orange)
- 2 Heavy duty snaps (⅝")
- Nighttime images

TOOLS
- Jumbo snap fastener tool kit

FOR TRAIN BAND:

1.0 Measure your wrist 2½" up from your hand and add 1".

2.0 Create 1 blue band with 3 strips based on that measurement.

3.0 Cut 1 strip of orange tape the length of your band and adhere it horizontally across the bottom. Leave a bit of blue showing along the edge.

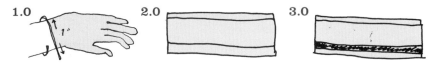

FOR TRAIN WINDOWS:

Cut 1½" x 2" white DT pieces (the quantity will depend on the length of your band). These will be your "canvases" for your nighttime scenes.

1.0

Option #1: Adhere different colored DT onto the white to "paint" a scene. (Ex: green grass, black mountains, blue sky, white moon and stars.)

Option #2: "Laminate" nighttime photos/color printout images using clear tape.

2.0 Round the corners of your windows and adhere them onto the blue strips above the orange strip.

3.0 Attach snaps.

clear tape

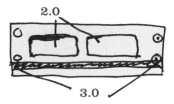

2.4 ✳✳✳✳
LIFER

Killer beats thump thump as Adia makes her way to the dance scene, styling. And by "dance scene" I mean bathroom. And by "killer beats" I mean someone's banging, hurry up.

MATERIALS

- DT (black, pink)
- Wire (18-gauge)

TOOLS

- Long needle nose pliers
- Wire cutter
- Silhouette template (see pg. 263)

1.0 With your hand palm-down, bend 1 piece of wire around your upper forearm from about seven o'clock to five o'clock. Cut the wire, but then keep it on your arm.

1.1 Bend 5 more pieces of wire in the same fashion, moving down your forearm, until the last one is around your wrist. Measure the distance between the first wire and the last.

1.2 Take the wires off of your arm, keeping them in order. Then create a loop at their ends with pliers.

2.0 Cut black strips (length = distance between first wire and last wire on your arm + 2"). Cut enough strips to create 1 sheet big enough to cover the longest wire.

2.1 With the first strip (SSU) you use to start your "fabric," leave one 1" margin on the LFT and RT sides and ½" at the top. Line up the wires in decreasing sizes, equal space apart. Then proceed to create your DT sheet as you usually would, sandwiching the wires between it.

3.0 When your sheet is complete, you will be able to see the wire shapes through the DT. Leave at least ¼" margin as you trim the edges, following the outer points of the wire.

4.0 Create and adhere "crime scene" silhouette onto the wrap, based on template. [see page 263]

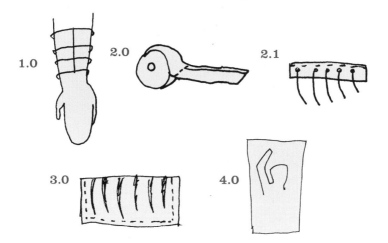

2.5 ✳✳✳✳
CHASER

Vinnie flags down gals (and some guys) with a quick flick of his wrist. Like him, you'll be such a hot rod. You know you will.

MATERIALS

- DT (black, red, white)
- 2 Heavy duty snaps (⅝")

TOOLS

- Jumbo snap fastener tool kit

Measure your wrist 1¾" up from your hand and add 1".

Create 1 black band with 2 strips at that measurement.

In addition, cut 1 white strip and 1 red strip at that same measurement and four 1" black pieces.

Hold your black band longwise and fold in half, E2E.

Create warp: Keep 1" margins at the top and bottom and ¼" along the bottom of your "sideways mountain." Within those margins, cut down the peak of the mountain horizontally every ½". Then unfold.

Create red and white weft: Work with 1 strip at a time SSU, with the SSB. SSS the LFT and RT sides to the middle.

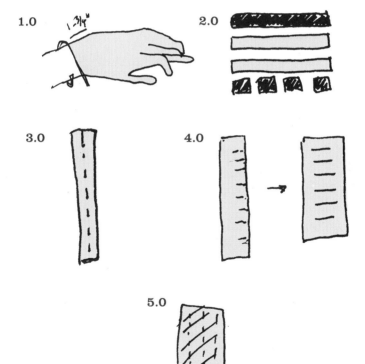

1.0 2.0

3.0 4.0

5.0

Cut down the V-axis.

To weave: Begin with the white weft and bring it up from the bottom of Slit 1. Then push it down through Slit 2. Repeat that pattern until it reaches the end. With the red weft, push it through the top of Slit 1 and pull it up through Slit 2. Repeat the pattern until the weave is complete.

To seal the weft in place, use the four 1" black strips. Line them up and place them over the wefts, front and back. Trim edges if necessary.

Attach snaps.

5.1

6.0

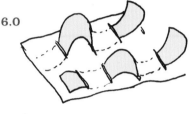

7.0

8.0

NOTES: ....

....

....

....

....

....

....

....

NOTES:

BLACK

Goth? Emo? New Yorker? [Insert stereotype here.] Then ignore it, like Eric. And wear this wicked wrap to represent instead.

MATERIALS

- DT (black)
- 2 Heavy duty snaps (⅝")

TOOLS

- Jumbo snap fastener tool kit

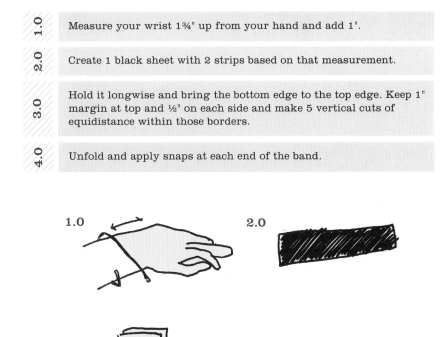

1.0 Measure your wrist 1¾" up from your hand and add 1".

2.0 Create 1 black sheet with 2 strips based on that measurement.

3.0 Hold it longwise and bring the bottom edge to the top edge. Keep 1" margin at top and ½" on each side and make 5 vertical cuts of equidistance within those borders.

4.0 Unfold and apply snaps at each end of the band.

1.0

2.0

3.0

4.0

NOTES:

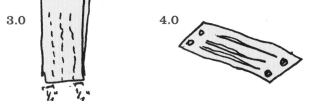

* * * *

HUNG UP

Back in the day, Sophie used to get wrapped up in phone calls . . . literally. Flaunt this funky one. But don't tell grandma.

MATERIALS
- DT (gray, other optional colors)
- Wire (18-gauge)

TOOLS
- Long needle nose pliers
- Wire cutter

1.0 Cut 1 arm's length of wire and make a loop at each end with pliers.

2.0 Cut an arm's length of gray DT and place it SSU on a flat surface, LSB. Stick the wire parallel to it on its top edge.

2.1 Roll the top edge of the DT over the wire and continue rolling until the wire is completely wrapped in it.

Decorative option: At this point if you want to wrap other colored tapes for decoration, do so.

3.0 To shape the DT wire into a bracelet, start with one end and wrap it around your index finger. Once you have no more room to wrap, slip off the wire (maintaining the curl shape) and continue to wrap around your finger where you left off. Repeat until the whole wire is curled.

4.0 For clasp: Form one end of the bracelet into a loop and the other into a hook. Insert the hook into the loop to clasp.

1.0

2.0

2.1

3.0

4.0

LOSER

As Sara sits on the couch, her 8-year-old cousin whips her the "L" against his forehead. She whips him her wrist, in return.

MATERIALS

- DT (red, gray)

1.0 Cut one 2" strip of red and gray DT. (Total quantity will depend on your wrist size.)

2.0 To create "L" links with sticky tabs:

(a.) SSU, fold LFT to RT, leaving one ¼" vertical margin on the RT.
(b.) Cut 1 "L" out of the piece. A small sticky tab on the bottom RT should remain.

3.0 Tabs SSU, stick together 1 gray "L" (right-side up) and 1 red "L" (upside down). This should create 1 "L" rectangle.

4.0 Interlink "L" rectangles together until bracelet is complete.

5.0 Bracelet closure: Like being labeled a "loser" can stick, so does this closure. Wrap the bracelet around your wrist and lock the last link into place with its sticky tab.

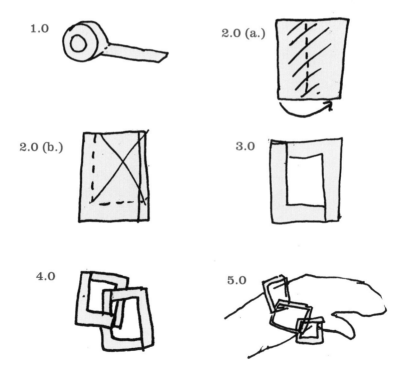

1.0

2.0 (a.)

2.0 (b.)

3.0

4.0

5.0

2.9 ✳✳✳✳
TELEPHONIC

Brigid demands to borrow this bracelet. But you hear from Carrie who heard from Sam that she's such a snappy witch—or did they mean her dog. They don't like her very much either.

MATERIALS
- DT (gray)
- Artist tape (½", baby-blue)
- Gaffers tape (1", black)
- Wire (18-gauge)

TOOLS
- Long needle nose pliers
- Wire cutter

1.0 Cut wire to about 1½ arm's length.

2.0 Create 1 loop at each end of the wire, using pliers.

3.0 Create wire skeleton: Start at your wrist and wrap one end of the wire once around it. Latch the wire through the loop at the under part of your forearm. Let the wire run down about 1" then wrap it around your arm again. When you return to the under part of your arm again, thread the wire underneath the wire that runs parallel with your arm. Repeat this step until you have wrapped all you can. Then latch the loop at the end of the wire.

4.0 Carefully remove the skeleton.

5.0 Cut tiny strips of various tape and wrap each one around the top portion of the skeleton to create a "flag" effect. Fill the whole top with flags.

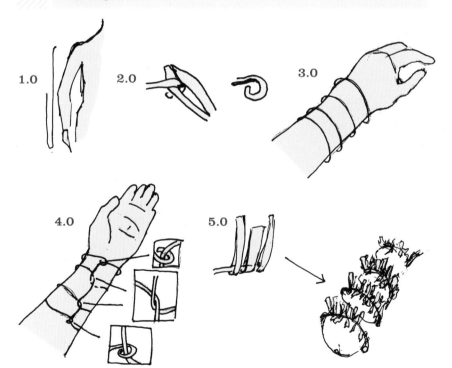

1.0   2.0   3.0

4.0   5.0

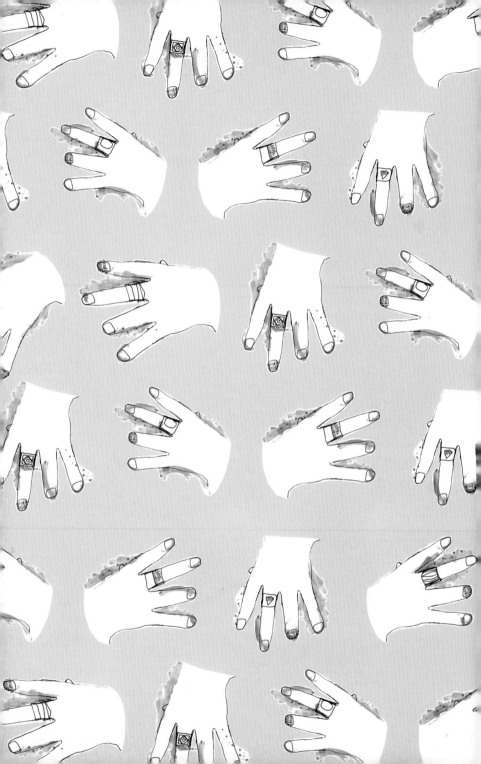

CHAPTER THREE

RINGS

SHERRY

Whether you're sipping Shirley Temples in the corner, like Hannah, or flaunting your slinky Red Dress in front of friends, like Wendy, let your lady ring sing, like Sherry.

MATERIALS
- DT (red, white)
- Transparent nylon thread
- Square bead (10mm)

TOOLS
- Hole punch
- Needle

1.0 Measure your "ring" finger with a piece of string and add ¼". Cut 1 strip of red DT to that measurement.

2.0 With the LSB, cut out 1 tiny vertical rectangle from the H-axis to the upper LFT corner. Repeat in the lower RT corner.

2.1 Fold in half along the H-axis, SSS, E2E.

Tip: To alter the thickness of the band, simply trim it horizontally

3.0 Keep the sticky tab SSU and punch an odd number of holes of equidistance along the middle of the band.

4.0 Cut 1" piece of white DT and fold it SSS, E2E. Then trim down to a ½" x ½" square.

1.0

2.0-2.1

3.0

4.0

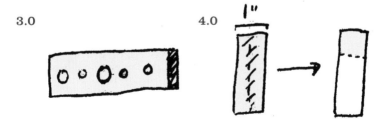

5.0 Thread a needle with 10" of string and knot together both ends of the thread, enough times so it won't slip through the DT, and leave 2" at the end.

6.0 Place the white square on top of the middle circle of the band. Insert the needle to the RT of the middle circle from the bottom. Sew through the band and white square and bead, then sew back down through the middle of the square, exiting through the middle hole of the band. Knot the strings together on the underside of the ring.

6.1 Cut 1 tiny red square to fit over the middle hole and keep the knotted strings in place.

7.0 Loop the band into a ring by overlapping the 2 sticky tabs, SSS.

5.0

6.0

6.1

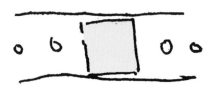

7.0

NOTES:

3.1 ✳✳✳✳
TAINTED

Brian gave her this ring, then dumped her for Kelly—or was it Dana?
One of those guy's names that's deceptive, like love.

MATERIALS

• DT (black, red)

1.0 Measure your "ring" finger with a piece of string and add ¼". Cut 1 strip of black DT to that measurement.

2.0 With the LSB, cut out 1 tiny vertical rectangle from the H-axis to the upper LFT corner. Repeat in the lower RT corner.

2.1 Fold in half along the H-axis, SSS, E2E.

Tip: To alter the thickness of the band, simply trim it horizontally.

3.0 Cut 1 strip of red DT about ⅓ the length of your black DT strip. Slice out 1 heart-shape from the middle of it. Discard the heart.

3.1 SSD, wrap the red strip around the black band.

4.0 Loop the band into a ring by overlapping the 2 sticky tabs, SSS.

1.0  **2.0** 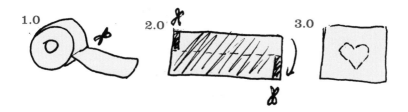 **3.0**

3.1

4.0

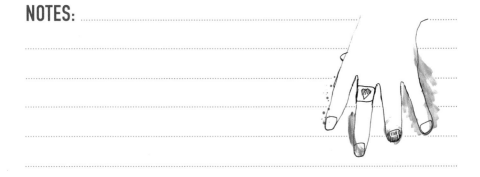

NOTES:

APOCALYPSE

Uncle Henry has a hankering for bad news—predicting the apocalypse by a message from Aunt Meg's muffins. By Taye's ring he predicts wolves howling the world's end.

MATERIALS

- DT (white, dark blue)
- Wire (24-gauge)

TOOLS

- Wire cutter

1.0	Measure your "ring" finger with a piece of string and add ¼". Cut 1 strip of blue DT to that measurement.
2.0	Cut 5 pieces of wire a little shorter than your DT.
2.1	With the DT LSB, SSU, place the wires parallel on the upper half of the strip. Keep 1 tiny margin at the top for fold-over.
2.2	Fold over the top margin. Then, fold the bottom half along the H-axis, SSS, E2E. Trim edges if necessary.
3.0	Cut 1 small circle "moon" out of white DT and adhere it to the middle of the band.
4.0	Bend the band into ring-shape.

1.0
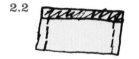

2.0

2.1

2.2

3.0

4.0

NOTES:

ELEMENTAL

Remember nights by the bonfire with buddies? Ahh, fresh air. Freedom. Jonesing for the rain, like Rain, so you could finally go home and make this ring.

MATERIALS

- DT (blue, orange)

1.0	Measure your "ring" finger with a piece of string and add ¼". Cut 1 strip of blue and 1 of orange DT to that measurement.
2.0	Both pieces SSD and LSB, layer the orange on top of the blue so there's about ¼" blue revealing on the LFT side and bottom.
3.0	About ¾" from the bottom, fold the piece back so the sticky sides touch.
4.0	Cut off the horizontal SSU portion.
5.0	Keep the orange and blue strips on the outside and join the 2 short ends, connecting the sticky tabs.

1.0   2.0   3.0

4.0   5.0

NOTES:

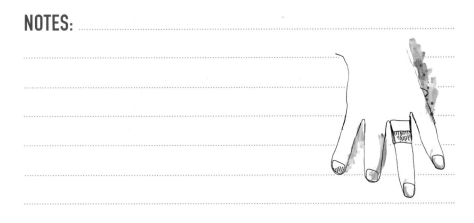

3.4 ✳✳✳✳
CRIMINAL

Cindy's klepto sister is all like, "I didn't steal your flippin' ring, leave me alone!" She pulls her hand from behind her back and she's all, "I'm just borrowing it!"

MATERIALS
- DT (white)
- Electric tape (¾", black)
- Wire (24-gauge, black)

TOOLS
- Wire cutter

| 1.0 | Measure your "ring" finger with a piece of string and add ¼". Cut 1 strip of white DT to that measurement. |

| 2.0 | With the LSB, cut out 1 tiny vertical rectangle from the H-axis to the upper LFT corner. Repeat in the lower RT corner. |

| 2.1 | Fold in half along the H-axis, SSS, E2E. |

Tip: To alter the thickness of the band, simply trim it horizontally.

| 3.0 | Cut at least 20 pieces of wire, long enough to wrap completely around your band short-wise. |

| 4.0 | Wrap each piece of wire around the band to create a "bar" effect. All ends should meet along the H-axis of one side. |

| 5.0 | Cut 1 strip of electric tape, long enough to cover the bar ends, but not the sticky tab. |

| 6.0 | Keep the black on the underside of the band when you loop it into a ring by overlapping the 2 sticky tabs, SSS. |

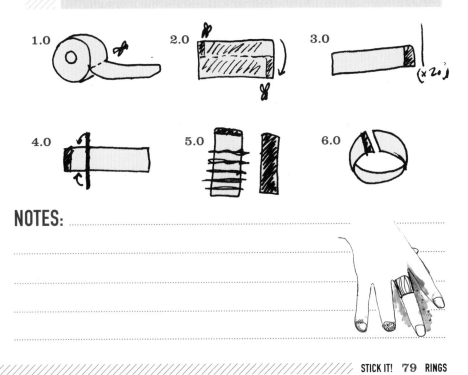

NOTES:

3.5 ✳✳✳✳
LOL

OMGYG2BK! Like Mia, you tell UR rents it's NOYB, YR BFF & U did it JFF. But U can't get out of it or say TLK2UL8R, so U LOL and say W/E instead.

MATERIALS
- DT (gray, white)

TOOLS
- Label maker

1.0 Measure your "ring" finger with a piece of string and add ¼". Cut 1 strip of gray DT to that measurement.

2.0 With the LSB, cut out 1 tiny vertical rectangle from the H-axis to the upper LFT corner. Repeat in the lower RT corner.

2.1 Fold in half along the H-axis, SSS, E2E.

Tip: To alter the thickness of the band, simply trim it horizontally.

3.0 Cut one 1" strip of white DT and wrap it around the middle of the gray band. Trim edges if necessary.

4.0 With label maker, create lettering: LOL!
Adhere to the front of the band on top of the white.

5.0 Loop the band into a ring by overlapping the 2 sticky tabs, SSS.

1.0

2.0
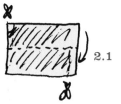
2.1

3.0
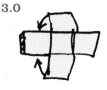

4.0

5.0

NOTES:

3.6

* * * *

POW

Madeline was a firecracker. She cheered sis-boom-bah and rah-rah-rah, until there was no more pow in her. She wore this ring all the time as a rah-rah reminder to keep positive.

MATERIALS

- DT (green, yellow, pink, red)
- Wire (24-gauge)

TOOLS

- Wire cutter

1.0 Cut one 4" strip of green DT and one 4" piece of wire. Then roll the wire in the DT.

2.0 To create "pow" petals, cut two 2" pieces of DT in yellow, pink, and red. Fold each piece SSS and leave a little sticky edge at the bottom.

2.1 Cut out a petal shape from each piece of DT. Make the yellow ones a little smaller than the others (they will be at the center of the flower).

3.0 Take the green stem and start to layer the petals around the top edge, pressing and scrunching the sticky part of the petals to the edge of the stem. Alternate and layer placement of petals. Start with yellow, then add pink, and then red.

4.0 Cut a thin piece of green DT and wrap it around the base of the petals to support their placement.

5.0 Wrap the stem around your finger to wear.

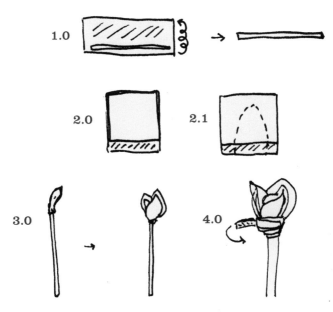

BLENDER

Samantha liked to mix things up and add a little sugar and spice to her worn-out wardrobe. She'd leave her room like hot cross buns out of an oven.

MATERIALS

- DT (black, pink)
- Wire (24-gauge))

TOOLS

- Wire cutter

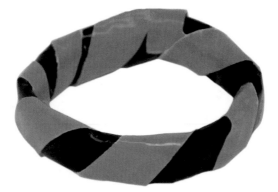

1.0	Measure your "ring" finger. Cut 1 strip of black DT and 1 strip of pink DT, plus 1 piece of wire based on that measurement.
2.0	Black piece SSU, LSB, place the wire parallel on the bottom edge and roll it in the tape.
3.0	From the pink, cut off 1 thin strip longwise. Wrap it around the black band.
4.0	Loop the band into a ring and wrap another piece of pink DT over the ends to seal.

1.0

2.0

3.0

4.0

NOTES:

CHAPTER FOUR

NECKLACES

H2O

You don't have to be a beach bum, like Blake, to make a splash with this necklace. Walk like you're on water . . . just don't feed the seagulls.

MATERIALS

- DT (royal blue)
- Transparent nylon thread
- Necklace clasp

TOOLS

- Hole punch

Measure yourself for a short necklace with a piece of string, then cut 1 strip of blue DT to that measurement.

SSB, fold it SSS along the V-axis, E2E.

Keep the fold on the LFT side and one 1" margin at the top and bottom. Cut a wavy ridge along the RT side. Then cut wavy "fringe" horizontally. Make sure not to cut through the left-hand fold.

Trim each end of the necklace by rounding the corners. Then punch a hole in the middle of the 1" margin and attach a clasp with clear thread.

1.0

2.0

3.0

4.0

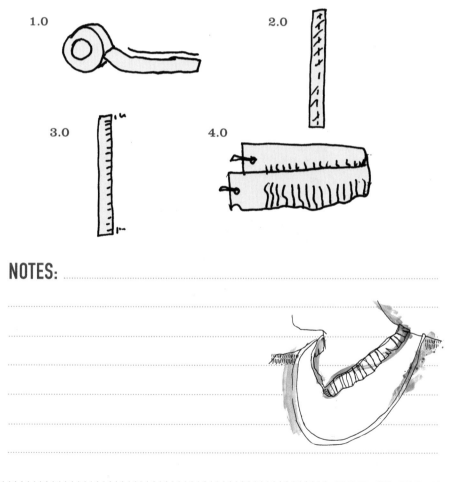

NOTES:

Five . . . four . . . three . . . two . . . one . . . Happy New Year! Love, Zay.
She sends you this necklace to wear every time you celebrate.

MATERIALS

- DT (silver)
- Transparent nylon thread
- Necklace clasp

TOOLS

- Small circle template (penny)

1.0 Cut one piece of thread to any desired length, plus a little extra to attach a clasp. Then cut one or two long strips of DT and place them on a cutting mat.

2.0 Use a penny (or anything else small and round) as a template. Place it on the DT and trace around it. Create multiple small circles and cut them out.

3.0 Fold each circle over the thread, placing them right next to each other, and alternating direction.

4.0 Attach necklace clasp and trim excess thread.

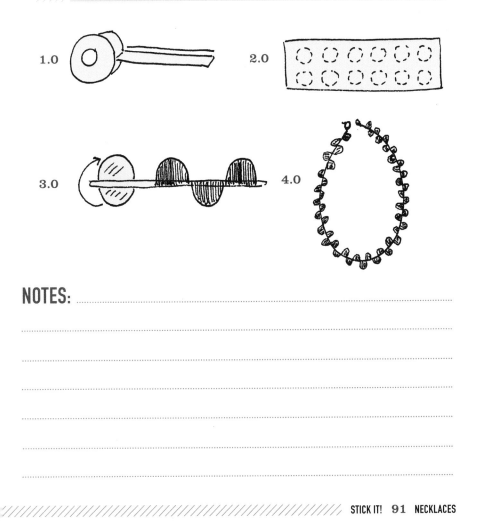

1.0

2.0

3.0

4.0

NOTES:

TUTTI-FRUTTI

Taryn's always hungry for eye candy. Wanting something a little healthier, she licked up this necklace. Just, you know, not literally.

MATERIALS
- DT (red, orange, pink, yellow)
- Transparent nylon thread
- Necklace clasp

TOOLS
- Hole punch (⅛")
- Circle template (plastic bottle cap)

1.0 Measure yourself for a medium-length necklace. Cut 1 thread to that length. Then, cut 1 thread, subtracting 2" from the original length. For the third thread, cut it to the second thread-length, minus 2". (Ex: 22", 20", 18")

1.1 Knot one end of all three threads to a necklace clasp.

2.0 Cut ten 2" squares out of each color.

2.1 Create little pieces of "fabric" by SSS 2 together. Repeat until you have 20 squares.

3.0 Use your circle template to trace and cut out circles from each square.

3.1 In the middle of each circle punch a hole.

4.0 Vary the color as you thread them onto each string of the necklace.

5.0 Knot the three loose ends together onto the remaining necklace clasp.

1.0
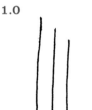

1.1

2.0

2.1

3.0

3.1

4.0

5.0

4.0
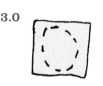

4.3 ✳✳✳✳
FOUND

Autumn's dad doesn't like to stop for directions. Her boyfriend doesn't either. And no matter where she is she feels lost, except when she wears this sign.

MATERIALS
- DT (white)
- Wire (18-gauge, black)
- Rub-on letters

TOOLS
- Long needle nose pliers
- Wire cutter
- Hole punch (⅛")
- Arrow-shaped template (see pg. 264)

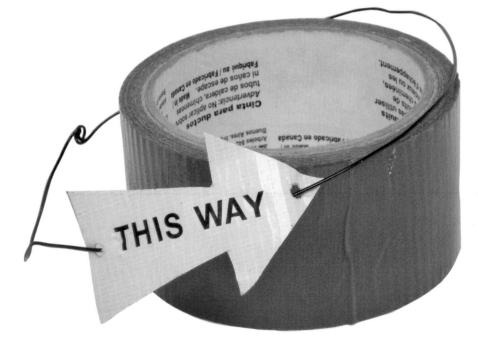

1.0	Create 1 white sheet by SSS two 3" strips together.
2.0	Trace the arrow-shape (based on the template) onto the sheet and cut it out.
3.0	Punch 1 hole at the point of the arrow and 1 hole at the opposite end.
4.0	Apply lettering: This Way
5.0	Measure yourself for a choker-necklace and cut wire based on that measurement.
5.1	Thread the wire into 1 hole, through the front of the sign, and out of the other.
6.0	Create a simple clasp by pinching one end of the wire between the pliers and rotating the wire once around it to make a loop.
6.1	To create the hook to latch into the loop, repeat Step 6, but do not close the loop.

2.0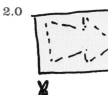

3.0

4.0

5.0 5.1

6.0

6.1

NOTES:

4.4 ✳✳✳✳
FLASH

Florence never imagined she'd collect so many pictures in her life. She could never choose which one to love more. But when she did, she wore it in this necklace.

MATERIALS
- DT (white)
- Wire (24-gauge, black)
- Photo/color copy of image
- Embroidery thread (black)

TOOLS
- Wire cutter
- Long needle nose pliers

1.0 Create one 2" white sheet. In addition, have one image cut a little smaller than that ready.

2.0 Create a second 2" white sheet, but before you seal the sides, place one 1" piece of wire formed into a loop-shape, using long needle nose pliers, at the middle of the top edge.

3.0 Cut a small square out of the white sheet that does not have the wire loop in it to create the frame. Leave more space on the bottom than the sides.

4.0 Place the frame on top of the wire-looped sheet. Seal the LFT, RT, and bottom sides with small strips of DT.

5.0 Place your photo in the frame through the top slit. String embroidery thread through the loop to complete the necklace.

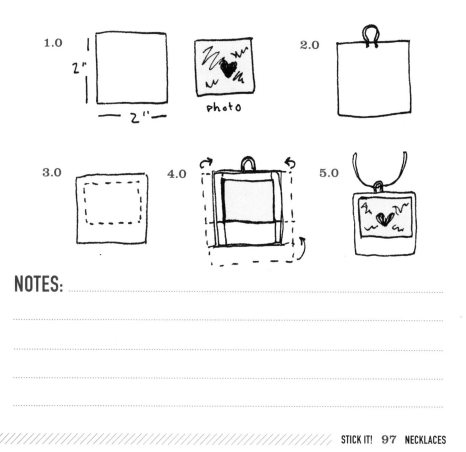

NOTES:

"Kelly?" "No . . . Kelli." That's what I said, Kelly." "No, it's Kelli, with an 'i.' You're saying Kelly with a 'y.'" "Oh." And she wore this necklace so everyone would know.

MATERIALS
- DT (any color)
- Wire (18-gauge, black)
- Template (cardstock)

TOOLS
- Long needle nose pliers
- Wire cutter

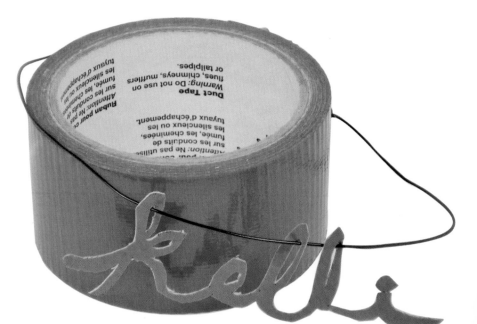

1.0 Create a nameplate template by drawing out your name, no higher than 2", on 1 piece of cardstock.

Tip: Make sure the letters are thick and connect to each other—take into consideration holes or loops for necklace wire/string.

2.0 Cut 1 strip of DT about 2 x the length of the name.

2.1 SSB, fold along the H-axis, SSS, E2E.

3.0 Trace the nameplate (based on the template) onto the sheet and cut it out.

4.0 Attach wire or string, threading it through the lettering (or through a hole at each end of the name), to complete the necklace.

1.0

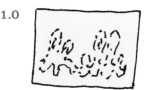

2.0

2.1

3.0

4.0

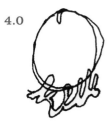

4.6 ✳✳✳✳
DOVE-CRY

As Opal sits in the park, a pigeon sulks over to her. She thinks it's because of her necklace. Really, it's because the others won't let him play.

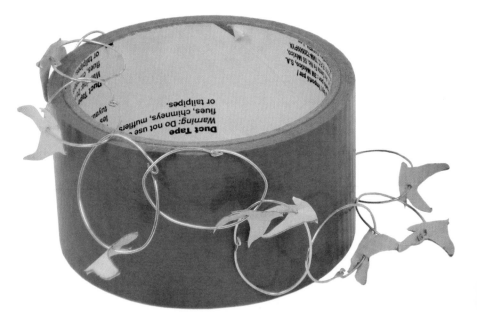

1.0 Shape individual large hoop ear wires into an oval and link them together temporarily to decide on the length of your necklace.

2.0 Cut 1 arm's length of DT and, LSB, fold it along the V-axis, SSS, E2E.

3.0 Trace the birds (based on the template) onto the sheet, cut them out, and poke a hole in them using a needle. (Allot for 1 bird per hoop.)

4.0 Thread each wire oval through 1 bird, then insert the straight end of the wire into the loop end and bend with pliers to close the link. Repeat, interlinking the wire ovals, but leave the last one open.

5.0 With the last link, do not bend the wire to a complete close. Instead, shape into an "L" to hook into the hole.

1.0   2.0   3.0

   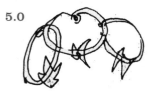

4.0   5.0

NOTES:

4.7 ✳✳✳✳
ETHEREAL

Gloria died and went to heaven, and when she got there God said, "Girl, take this necklace, wear it, and live in it." And back to Earth she fell.

MATERIALS

MATERIALS

- DT (yellow, white)
- Transparent nylon thread
- Necklace clasp

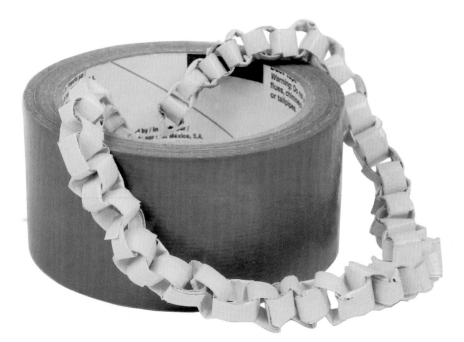

For necklace links: Cut ½" strips of yellow and white DT. (Quantity will depend on how long you want your necklace.)

1.0
(a.) Take each strip, SSB and SSU, and cut along the V-axis from the bottom about ⅓ of the way up.
(b.) Flip up the LFT flap, SSS. Then flip it over to the RT, E2E.
(c.) What remains should be 1 fabric band with a sticky tab.

2.0
Create 1 ring with the band by overlapping and sealing the ends together, tab SSD.

3.0
Link rings together in a "chain," alternating colors, until you reach your desired necklace length.

4.0
At each end of the necklace, attach a clasp and tag with clear thread.

(a.)   (b.)   (c.)

1.0

2.0   3.0   4.0

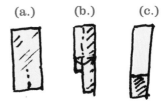

NOTES:

4.8 ✳✳✳✳

UNBREAKABLE

Tightrope-walking Tara lived on the edge of everything, wearing this. She liked it that way, living on the fast path from point A to point B.

MATERIALS

- DT (black, brown, white, gray)
- Necklace clasp

1.0	Measure yourself for a medium-length necklace. Cut 1 thread to that length. Then, cut 1 thread, subtracting 2" from the original length. For the third thread, cut it to the second thread-length, minus 2". (Ex: 22", 20", 18")
1.1	Knot one end of all 3 threads to a necklace clasp.
2.0	Cut one 8" strip of DT in each color.
2.1	LSB, SSU, cut out a triangle.

Tip: Make 1 slice from the bottom LFT corner to the top middle, then from the bottom RT to the top middle.

3.0	Work with 1 piece of string and DT SSU at a time. Place the string along the long edge, leaving a little space at the bottom for fold-over.
3.1	Fold the bottom edge of the tape over the string and continue to roll until the DT is completely rolled up.
4.0	Repeat Steps 3.0-3.1 for the others.
5.0	Knot the 3 loose ends together onto the remaining necklace clasp.

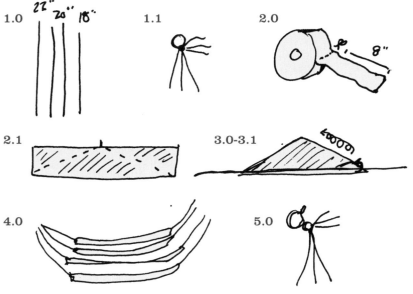

1.0   22"   20"   18"   1.1   2.0   8"

2.1   3.0-3.1

4.0   5.0

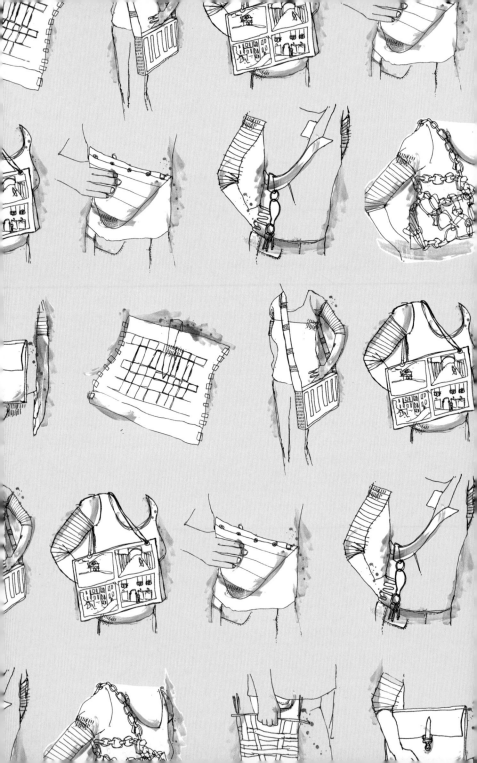

CHAPTER FIVE

BAGS & PURSES

5.0 ✳✳✳✳
PLAYER

Alone Sicily sat, spilling out the contents of her purse: lipstick, cash, peppermints, car key, and a napkin reading 555-5683.

- DT (brown, pink, purple)

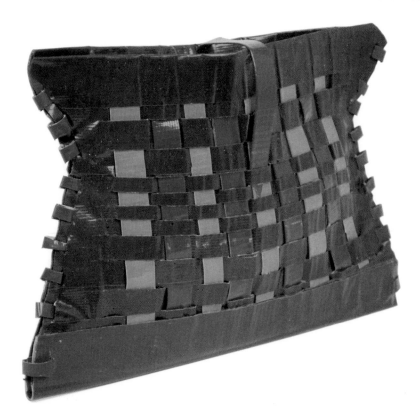

FOR PURSE WALLS AND WARP:

1.0   Create 2 brown sheets 5½" x 9". LSB.

2.0   For each sheet, on the LFT side, measure down 2" from the top and 1" from the LFT edge—mark that spot. Then cut from the upper and lower LFT corners to that spot. Repeat the same process on the RT side.

3.0   Keep 1" margins around the perimeter and make horizontal slices within that border that will create varying warp thicknesses (¼"-½").

1.0   (x2)   2.0   3.0

FOR WEFT:

1.0   Cut:
- Five 5½" pink DT strips
- Four 5½" purple DT strips

2.0   Work with 1 strip at a time SSU, with the SSB. SSS the LFT and RT sides to the middle.

2.1   Cut down the V-axis. You should end up with 18 strips total.

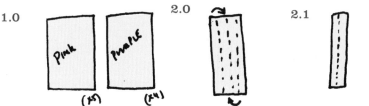

1.0   pink (x5)   purple (x4)   2.0   2.1

FOR WEAVING PURSE WALLS:

1.0

Begin with the pink weft and bring it up from the bottom of Slit 1.
Then push it down through Slit 2. Repeat that pattern until it
reaches the end. With the purple weft, push it through the top of
Slit 1 and pull it up through Slit 2. Repeat the pattern until the
weave is complete.

2.0

To seal the weft in place, wrap one 9" brown strip over each side.
Trim edges.

1.0  2.0

FOR CONNECTING PURSE WALLS:

1.0

SSB, lay the 2 walls so they mirror each other and the sides you
want to be "inside" are face up. Keep about ½" between the 2 sheets.

1.1

Cut two 9" purple strips and place 1 SSD over the 2 vertical edges in
the middle. Turn the whole sheet over and stick the second strip down
the same way, aligning it with the other. Trim edges when complete.

2.0

Bring both walls together and make at least 9 slices about ¼" long
and ¼" from the LFT and RT side edges.

1.0-1.1  2.0

To create DT links (to connect the sides together): Cut eighteen ½" purple strips.

(a.) Take each strip, SSB and SSU, and cut along the V-axis from the bottom about half of the way up.

(b.) Flip up the LFT flap, SSS. Then flip it over to the RT, E2E.

(c.) What remains should be 1 fabric band with 1 sticky tab.

Slip each link through a slit—trim each link to keep the walls snug—and SSS the tab to the other end of the band to seal.

To create a small flap closure over the top of the purse:

Make one 7" purple weft. Trim the bottom into the shape of a triangle tip and attach the square end into the inside middle top of the purse. Tuck that end into a purple weave, and cut 1 small strip of brown DT to the size of a small warp section (about 2" x ½") to secure it. Fold over the purple "clasp" and weave it into the front of the purse.

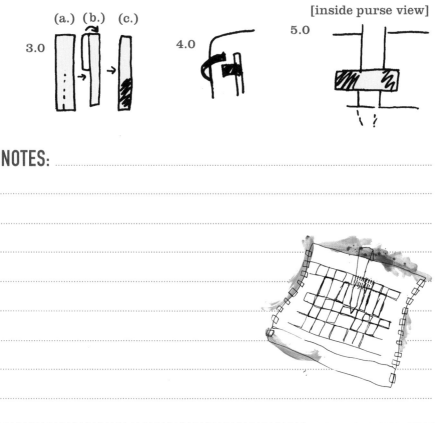

(a.) (b.) (c.)

3.0

4.0

[inside purse view]

5.0

NOTES:

5.1 ✳✳✳✳
GRAND

Clause von Viper could never disengage from the little black notes that followed him everywhere. He even tried to shove them in this bag.

MATERIALS
- DT (black, white, gray)
- Electric tape (black)
- Mailing box (18" x 12½" x 3")
- Large brown grocery bag

TOOLS
- Utility knife

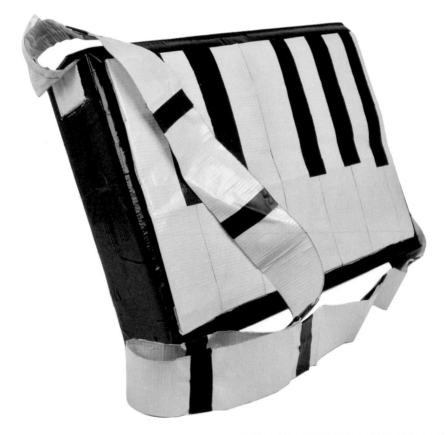

Mailing box SSB:

(a.) Measure up from the bottom 9" on the front and 2 sides—slice horizontally.

(b.) Measure up from the bottom 12" on the back—slice horizontally. Then cut vertically along the LFT and RT sides to the bottom.

Open up the box to lay flat—this will be the inside of your bag. To create the spine of the bag flap, measure 3" from the top and lightly score horizontally. Cover the entire "inside" with gray DT—LFT to RT, bottom to top. Allot ½" for edge-wrap-around. (Exclude the 2 small tabs on the LFT and RT and the top flap spine.)

To create the bag flap: Cut and discard the bottom and top off of a large brown grocery bag while it's folded flat. Trim the rest of the bag to 10" x 12", keeping the paper doubled. Attach this to the inside of the flap spine on the box, overlapping it 1". Tape over it horizontally and finish covering the rest of the flap with gray DT.

Pull the LFT and RT spines of the bag to the interior, folding in the uncovered tabs as well. With 2 gray strips, cover those tabs to lock them in place.

To seal the bag into its shape, pull the back side up to join the spine edges. Lock the 3 sides into place—first wrap black strips horizontally around the spines, overlapping the front and back of the bag by at least ½".

Once the sides and bottom are sealed, cover the front and back with 12" black strips.

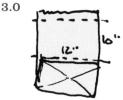

(a.)   (b.)

2.0

3.0   4.0   5.0-5.1

6.0 Cover the bag's top flap spine with horizontal black strips as well.

6.1 To create "piano keys" on the front flap:
(a.) Adhere vertical white strips next to each other until the flap is covered front and back.
(b.) Cut three 5" black strips. SSB, cut each piece along the V-axis. Then stick vertically, from the bag flap spine, along the first, second, fourth, fifth, and sixth white strip crease.

7.0 For bag strap: Cut one 2" slot in the LFT and RT sides. Make the slice 1" from the top and ½" from the edges.

7.1 Work with one arm's length of white tape at a time. LSB, SSS each piece along the V-axis. Attach pieces together by sandwiching overlapping ends. With the first and last strips, keep one 6" sticky tab to later loop through the slots on the sides.

7.2 Once the strap is complete, slip the tab SSU through each slot and SSS to the underside of the strap.

7.3 Decorative option: Wrap strips of black electric tape around the crease lines to conceal where the white pieces join.

6.1 — (b.) (a.)

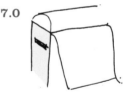

7.0

7.1

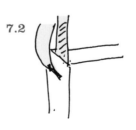

7.2

7.3

NOTES:

5.2 ✳✳✳✳
FOREIGNER

Bernadette bellowed: Memory carriers huddle around! Watch closely as we turn your moments in time into something sublime!

MATERIALS
- DT (red)
- Grommets
- Double-stick tape
- Travel photos

TOOLS
- Grommet setter

- Two 12" x 9" sheets (LSB, bag front + back)
- Two 9" x 2" sheets (SSB, bag sides)
- One 12" x 12" sheet (bottom)
- Four 1" x 12" strips (sealing strips)
- Four 1" x 9" strips (sealing strips)
- Two 1" x 1¾" (sealing strips)
- Two 30" x ½" (bag straps)

1.0 Apply double-stick tape to the back of photos and adhere them to one 12" x 9" sheet.

Tip: Seal their edges with DT to insurse they stick.

2.0 On a flat surface, align the following sheets in a column (from the top to bottom) E2E (face out):
- One 12" x 9" (photo-covered front)
- One 12" x 2"
- One 12" x 9"

Along each seam, adhere one 1" x 12" strip, SSD.

3.0 Place one 9" x 2" sheet to the RT of the photo sheet and the other to the LFT of it. Align the edges and seal each vertical seam with one 1" x 9" strip.

4.0 Attach grommets to the upper LFT and RT corners of the photo sheet and in the lower LFT and RT corner of the bottom large rectangle.

5.0 Fold the purse into its 3-D form and seal the LFT, RT, and bottom edges of the sides of the bag with strips of coinciding lengths.

6.0 Attach 30" x ½" straps through the grommets and knot each end inside.

1.0

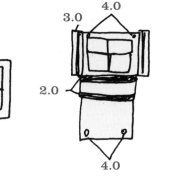

3.0 **4.0** **2.0** **4.0**

6.0

PARANOID

Keys? Check. Wallet? Check. Phone? Check. Purse sealed so no psycho stranger can steal every ounce of Claudine's life? Check.

MATERIALS
- DT (black)
- 5-buttons
- Thread

TOOLS
- Needle

DT COMPONENTS:

- One 11" x 9" sheet (LSB, purse front)
- One 11" x 9" sheet with 1" SSU margin at top (LSB, purse back)
- Five ⅛" x 3" SSS strips (loops for closure)
- Eighteen to twenty 1" x 1" strips (sealing strips)

1.0 With the purse-back sheet, make 1" horizontal slices every other inch, along the border of the sticky edge.

2.0 Make "ribbon" loops: With each ⅛" x 3" piece, cross the LFT end over the RT. Then feed each loop through the front of 1 slice so the feet of the ribbon hang out a bit.

2.1 Fold the top flap over, SSS, sandwiching the ribbon feet into place.

3.0 Place the purse front on top of the purse back. Carefully holding them aligned, trim them into the shape of a bottom of a strawberry, rounding the top corners, too.

4.0 1" down from the top, begin wrapping the 1" x 1" strips around the edges to seal the front and back together. Continue and stop on the other side 1" from the top, as you started.

5.0 Sew 5 buttons onto the front of the purse, along the top 1" horizontal margin line. Make sure they line up with the ribbon loops.

6.0 To close the purse, tuck the 1" margin down towards the inside of the purse and fold the back flap over the front, latching the loops around the buttons.

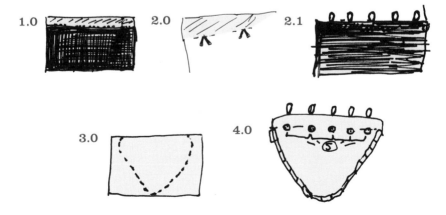

1.0   2.0   2.1

3.0   4.0

5.4 **** FREAKSTER

Chuck's such a freak. I mean, he's the freakiest of the freaks. He's a super freak. He's what little freaks want to be when they grow up and wear stuff like this.

MATERIALS

- DT (black)
- Steel split ring
- Adhesive Velcro

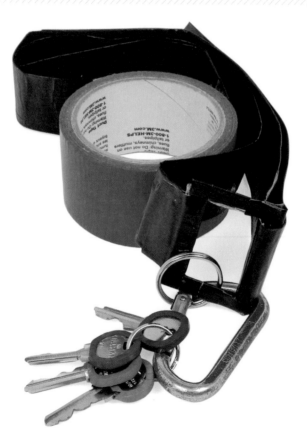

DT COMPONENTS:

- 3 arm-length SSS strips (more or less, depending on your body-type)
- Buckle (see pg. 148 ["Respect"], Step 2.0)

1.0 Connect 3 strips: Wrap 1 thick strip of DT around each connecting point.

2.0 To create a hidden pocket (for cash): Cut one 4" x 1¾" sheet. LSB, cut one 3" slit along the H-axis. Attach it to the middle of the 3 strips and seal the edges with ½" strips of DT.

3.0 Add 1 sticky tab, SSD, to the end of the last strip on the RT. Create 1 buckle and attach it by inserting the tab through it and SSS it to the band.

4.0 With the hidden pocket on the inside, wrap the band diagonally across your shoulder and chest and under your opposite arm. Loop one end of the band through the buckle. (Trim the band—or add to it—at this point, if necessary.) Then adhere Velcro to the underside of the band you just pulled through the buckle and the other side of the Velcro to the outer part of the band.

5.0 Attach the steel split ring to the buckle.

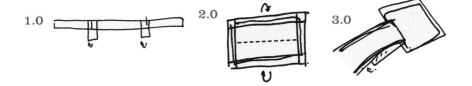

1.0   2.0   3.0

4.0

5.0

CHAINED

Ruth runs a tight ship as a DT Craftster. "Work it!" she says. "Work it!" A prisoner of her own creation, she calls on your perseverance to make this one work.

MATERIALS

- DT (yellow, grass-green, white)

FOR PURSE-SKELETON LINKS:

Cut:
- Forty-two 3" green strips
- Twenty-two 3" yellow strips
- Thirty-eight 6" white strips

(a.) Take each strip, SSB and SSU, and cut along the V-axis from the bottom about ½" up.

(b.) Flip up the LFT flap, SSS. Then flip it over to the RT, E2E.

(c.) Cut down the V-axis. What remains should be 2 fabric bands with 1 sticky tabs.

Create 1 ring with 1 band by overlapping and sealing the ends together, tab SSD.

Link rings together in a "chain": Connect twenty-two 3" green rings to twenty-two 3" yellow ones, alternating colors. This will be the upper "rim" of your purse.

To begin creating a "net" off of the rim, connect one 6" white ring off of each green link.

Connect every 2 white rings with 1 additional 3" green ring. Continue this pattern around the rim.

Continuing down the "net," attach 1 white ring through 1 green ring. Continue the pattern around the net until all the links you cut are connected.

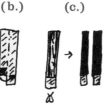

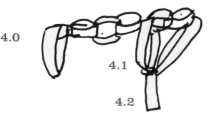

FOR PURSE INTERIOR:

DT COMPONENTS:

- One 16" x 10" yellow sheet (SSB)
- Two 3¾" x 2" yellow sheets (SSB)
- Two 2" x ½" yellow strips
- Four 3¾" x ½" yellow strips

1.0 Fold the large sheet so the height of 1 side equals 3¾", with the bottom width being 2". Attach the 2" x 3¾" sheets to the sides by wrapping the coinciding strips around the edges.

2.0 Cradle the yellow purse interior in the chain skeleton. Create purse handles to your desired length, by interlinking more 3" green and yellow rings.

1.0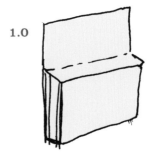

2.0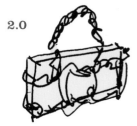

NOTES:

NOTES:

5.6 ✳✳✳✳
LIBERTY

Lucy let her feathered friend venture into freedom, through the window of her apartment. But the freedom Lucy loved to experience meant spending the coins at the bottom of her bag.

MATERIALS

- DT (royal-blue, brown, grass-green, yellow)
- 8 tree-sticks/cinnamon-sticks (12")

FOR PURSE SIDES:

1.0 Lay down 2 sticks vertically, about 8½" apart. On top of those place 2 other sticks horizontally about 9" apart.

2.0 Cut 10" strips of DT (4 brown, 4 yellow, 6 green, 6 blue).
- (a.) Take each strip, SSB and SSU, and cut along the V-axis from the bottom and top about 1" towards the center.
- (b.) Flip over the top and bottom LFT flaps, SSS. Then flip it over to the RT, E2E.
- (c.) What remains should be 1 fabric band with 2 sticky tabs.

3.0 Attach the 20 strips to the sticks accordingly (staying within the stick borders):
- (a.) Wrap the ends of the brown and yellow strips front to back around the top and bottom sticks. Attach the brown strips first to the outer edges. Then stick the yellow strips right next to the brown ones. The space LFT in the middle of the top horizontal sticks will be the handle.
- (b.) About 1½" from the top, wrap the green band tabs over and around the LFT vertical stick. Weave the strip under the brown and over the yellow and attach it to the RT vertical stick.
- (c.) Below the green band, wrap the blue strip tab under and around the LFT vertical stick. Weave the strip over the brown and under the yellow and attach the end to the RT vertical stick.
- (d.) Repeat green, blue, green, blue to complete the weave.

4.0 Repeat Steps 1.0-3.0 to complete Side 2 of the purse.

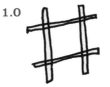

1.0

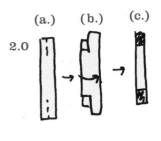

2.0 (a.) (b.) (c.)

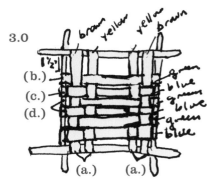

3.0

FOR PURSE POUCH INSIDE:

Cut brown strips:
- Four 12"
- Fourteen 8"
- Two 6"

(a.) Begin with one 12" strip SSU. Continue by layering seven 8" strips SSS, as if making a DT sheet. Then vertically trim ½" on each side of the fabric and 1" horizontally off of each side of the 12" strip.

(b.) Continue adding to that fabric by placing one 12" strip down, SSU, then layer one 8" strip on top of it. Once again, vertically trim ½" on each side of the fabric and 1" horizontally off of each side of the 12" strip.

(c.) Continue with the same sheet. Place down another 12" strip, this time SSD, then layer another 8" strip. Continue SSS with the 8" strips until you have no more left, then end the fabric with a 12" strip SSD. Trim as you did in a. and b.

Bring the bottom and top E2E—be careful that the 12" strip sticky tabs don't stick together. Use the two 6" strips to wrap around and seal the LFT and RT sides between the two 12" strips.

Sandwich the brown pouch between Side 1 and Side 2 stick pieces. Keep the horizontal sticks on the outside. Wrap the tabs of the brown pouch around the sticks to hold its place. Seal the bottom 2 holes on each side with brown DT.

1.0

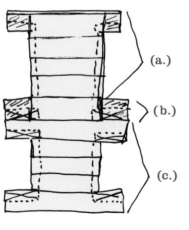

(a.)

(b.)

(c.)

2.0

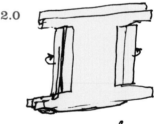

3.0

NOTES:

5.7 ✳✳✳✳
CHARITY

Raven loves to give stuff away. She gave away her cat in return for a really cool hat. And she gave away her brother, such a nag, for (you guessed it) this awesome bag.

MATERIALS

- DT (dark-blue)
- Overall button with no-sew button
- Cardboard (⅛" thick, 21" x 14½")

1.0 For cardboard case base: With the SSB, measure up from the bottom 6½", 7½", 16", and 17½"—mark and score horizontally to create folds at those points.

2.0 Begin covering the inside with DT, from the bottom to the top. Make sure that the DT overlaps the edges at least ½".

Tip: For covering corners with DT, make a ⅛" cut on each side of the corner. Fold the square over the corner and then fold in the other sides.

3.0 To close the sides: Cut four 6½" strips. Place 2 aside and then from the 6½" mark to the bottom stick the other 2 on each side with about 1½" hanging off the sides.

3.1 Fold the bottom up and attach the other sticky side of that DT to the inside of what will be the back wall of the case. Since you now have one 1" sticky spine on each side, use the other two 6½" strips to cover each side.

4.0 Proceed to cover the outside of the purse. (Leave the front flap for last.)

4.1 Cut one 7" strip and SSB, fold at the ½" point, then fold along the V-axis to create one ¾" strap.

4.2 Cut a "V" at the end of the strap. Attach the square end to the middle of the purse flap at the original 17½" point. Finish covering the rest of the flap, excluding the strap.

5.0 Attach overall button to finish closure.

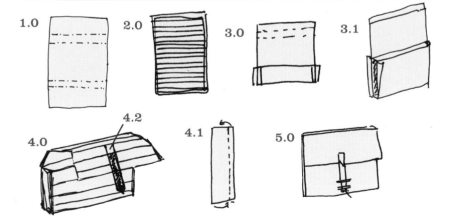

CHAPTER SIX

WILD WEARABLES

6.0 ✳✳✳✳

REBEL

Racing down the road going 103mph to a party, Zac's tie catches the wind. Later on it'll be letting loose, burning rubber on the dance floor.

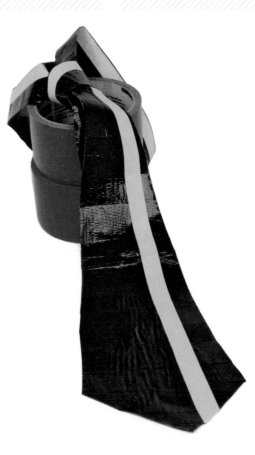

Create one 5" x 4¾' black sheet (SSB).

Use a tie as your pattern—or if you are familiar with how a tie looks, wing it—trace its shape onto the long fabric. Then cut around the tracing.

Adhere yellow tape vertically along the RT side of the tie and trim the excess at the top and bottom.

To create loop for the back of the tie: Cut one 1¾" strip of black DT.
(a.) SSB and SSU, and cut along the V-axis from the bottom and top about ¼" towards the center.

(b.) Flip over the top and bottom LFT flaps, SSS. Then flip it over to the RT, E2E.
(c.) What remains should be 1 fabric band with 2 sticky tabs. LSB, adhere the band at the 8½" point, measuring from the bottom of the tie.

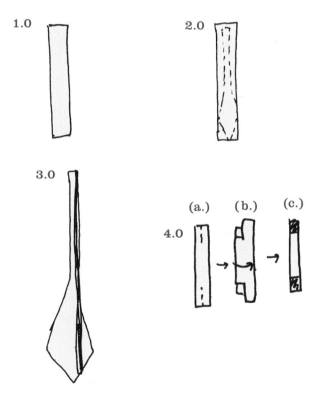

1.0

2.0

3.0

(a.) (b.) (c.)

4.0

Smooth jazz oozes out of Rob's skin—Armstrong, Coltrane, Holiday, Parker, and more. This tie is his tune.

MATERIALS

- DT (black, dark blue, white)

TOOLS

- Tie pattern

1.0 Create one 5" x 4¾' white sheet (SSB).

2.0 Use a tie as your pattern—or if you are familiar with how a tie looks, wing it—trace its shape onto the long fabric, but square off the bottom. Then cut around the tracing.

3.0 Cut zigzag "lightning bolts"—1 black and 1 blue—out of strips of DT and adhere to the LFT side of the tie.

4.0 To create loop for the back of the tie: Cut one 1¾" strip of black DT.
(a.) SSB and SSU, and cut along the V-axis from the bottom and top about ¼" towards the center.
(b.) Flip over the top and bottom LFT flaps, SSS. Then flip it over to the RT, E2E.
(c.) What remains should be 1 fabric band with 2 sticky tabs. LSB, adhere the band at the 8½" point, measuring from the bottom of the tie.

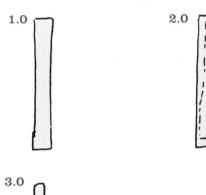

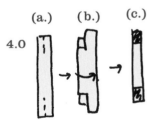

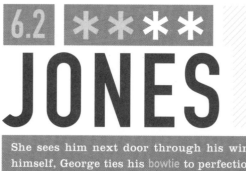

6.2 ✳✳✳✳
JONES

She sees him next door through his window every night. Primping himself, George ties his bowtie to perfection. How she wishes she had a man like that.

MATERIALS

- DT (black)

TOOLS

- Tie pattern

1.0 To measure for your bowtie: Hang a string/tape-measure around your neck—let one end hang at chest level and match the other end to that one. Create a black sheet (that length x 3" high).

2.0 Use a bowtie as your pattern—or if you are familiar with how a bowtie looks, wing it—trace its shape onto the long fabric.

3.0 Cut around the tracing.

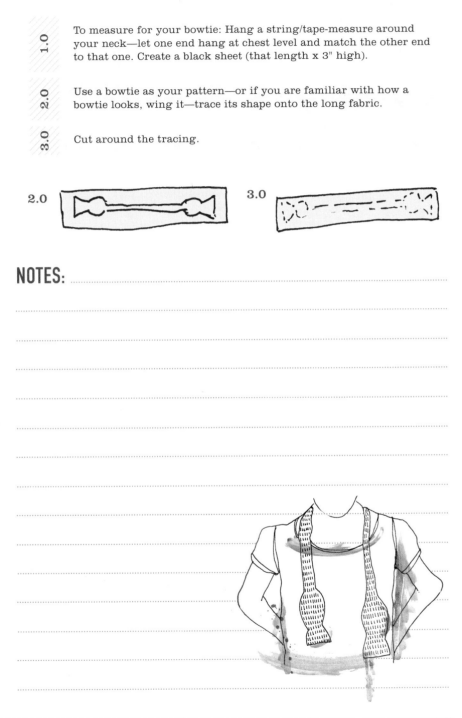

2.0

3.0

NOTES:

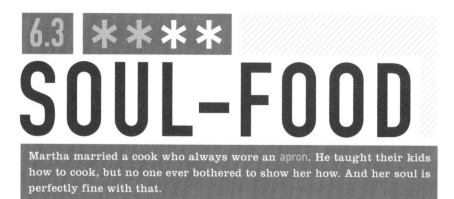

6.3 ✳✳✳✳
SOUL-FOOD

Martha married a cook who always wore an apron. He taught their kids how to cook, but no one ever bothered to show her how. And her soul is perfectly fine with that.

- DT (gray, white)

Create 1 gray sheet to your desired apron size. (Note: This design is not intended to wrap around the neck, but around the waist.) Keep one 1" sticky margin at the top of the fabric, which will be used to sandwich your DT strings.

To make apron strings: measure around your waist plus 2'. SSU, join long white strips together and fold longwise. Then trim the strip to ¼" wide. Place the string horizontal along the sticky margin of the apron and fold the top lip of the apron over it.

Decorate the front of your apron with various tapes to your soul's content.

Decoration option: use dove-template (see pg. 264), blown up to a larger size, to create a white DT dove to adhere to the apron.

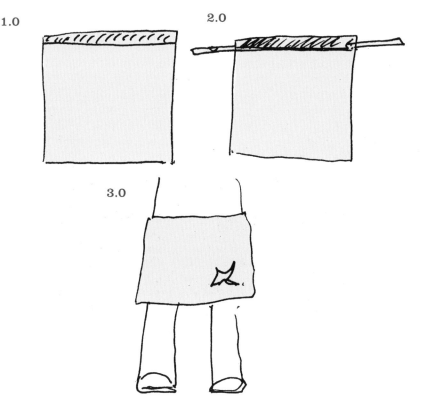

1.0

2.0

3.0

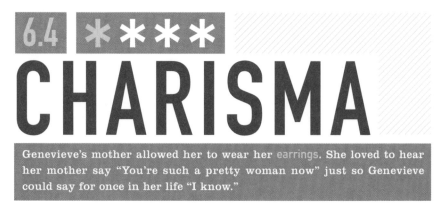

CHARISMA

Genevieve's mother allowed her to wear her earrings. She loved to hear her mother say "You're such a pretty woman now" just so Genevieve could say for once in her life "I know."

MATERIALS
- DT (red)
- Fish hook earrings (1")

TOOLS
- Earring template (see pg. 263)
- Hole punch (⅛")

1.0 Cut two 4" red strips.

2.0 SSB, SSU fold each strip SSS along the H-axis into a square.

3.0 Trace the earring pattern (based on the template) onto each sheet and cut them out.

3.1 Punch 1 hole in the top of them.

4.0 Attach 1 hook through the hole of each earring.

1.0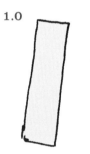

2.0

3.0 3.1

4.0

NOTES:

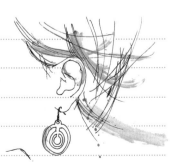

GLAMOROUS

When Maxine's girlfriends see these earrings they think they know what they are. Magazines think they know, too. Guys kind of have a clue. You know it because you are it.

MATERIALS
- DT (grass-green)
- Fish hook earrings (1")

TOOLS
- Earring template (see pg. 263)
- Hole punch (⅛")

Cut two 4" red strips.

SSB, SSU fold each strip SSS along the H-axis into a square.

Trace the earring pattern (based on the template) onto each sheet and cut them out.

Punch 1 hole in the top of them.

Attach 1 hook through the hole of each earring.

1.0

2.0

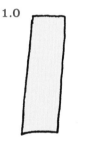

3.0

3.1

4.0

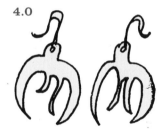

NOTES:

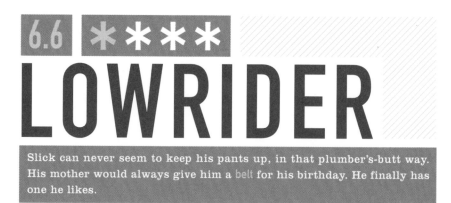

6.6 ✳✳✳✳ LOWRIDER

Slick can never seem to keep his pants up, in that plumber's-butt way. His mother would always give him a belt for his birthday. He finally has one he likes.

- DT (black)
- Overall button with no-sew button

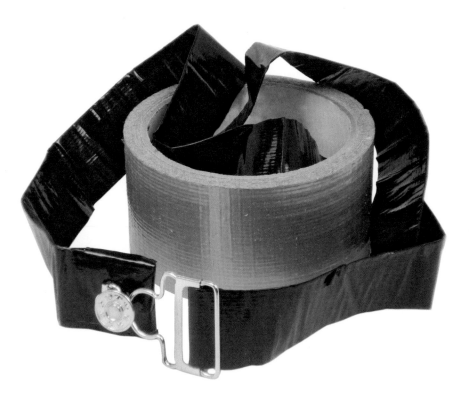

- Option #1: Use a belt you own as a template.
- Option #2: Measure your waste with a string/tape measure plus 6"

1.0 Create 1 black fabric strip that is 1" wide and to your belt-length.

2.0 Loop one end through an overall clasp, which will be the end you can adjust.

2.1 Attach the overall button about 1½" from the edge of the opposite belt-end. Then fold the belt-end to the back and secure its edges with strips of DT.

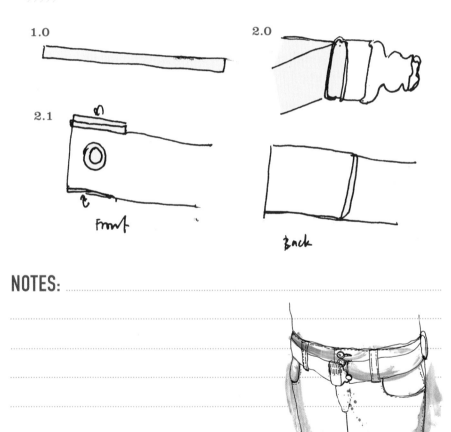

1.0

2.0

2.1

Front

Back

NOTES:

6.7 ✳✳✳✳
RESPECT

A girl's gotta know how to give and take respect. When Jo was little she loved to sing it and spell it out. She still likes to and wears this belt to remind others what she demands.

MATERIALS
- DT (black, white)
- Cardboard (3" x 3")
- Adhesive letters

TOOLS
- Utility knife

Create 1 black fabric strip that's as wide as the DT and to your belt-length. Keep one 1½" sticky tab at one end.

To create the belt buckle: Cut one 2¼" x 1¾" cardboard rectangle with one ¼" frame. Cover it with black strips.

To create the loop for the inside of the buckle:

Cut one 5" black strip of DT.

(a.) SSB and SSU, and cut along the V-axis from the bottom and top about ½" towards the center.
(b.) Flip over the top and bottom LFT flaps, SSS. Then flip it over to the RT, E2E.
(c.) What remains should be 1 fabric band with 2 sticky tabs.

With the belt buckle SSB, wrap the sticky-tab-band SSD around the top and bottom of the belt buckle so the tabs SSS with the loop, not the buckle. Once it's attached, slice the loop longwise in half.

To attach the belt to the buckle, feed the sticky tab (SSD) through the front of the buckle along one side and SSS to the belt (not the buckle).

Along the front side that you just attached, apply lettering: RESPECT

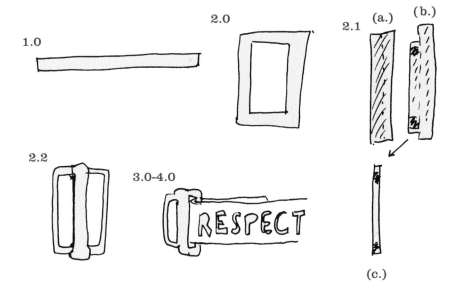

1.0

2.0

2.1 (a.) (b.)

2.2

3.0-4.0

RESPECT

(c.)

6.8 ✱✱✱✱
JUPITER

Dion used to say she saw Jupiter in Destiny's eyes. Was it their color, what did that mean? So she left Destiny a hatpin, a metaphoric dream.

MATERIALS

- DT (black, purple, white)
- Hat pin with cap

- One 1" x 1" gray strip
- Four 2½" purple DT fabric
- Four 2½" black DT fabric
- Four 2½" white DT fabric
- Four 2½" gray DT fabric
- One 3" x ¼" gray strip

1.0 With the 1" x 1" square SSU, make 1 diagonal cut from each corner and stop half way to the center. Then adhere to the top of your hat pin and wrap the edges around the pin.

2.0 Cut 1 long teardrop-shape out of each 2½" fabric strip.

3.0 Gather the teardrop ends around the bottom of the gray DT pin top, then wrap the 3" x ¼" strip around the ends and the pin to keep them in place.

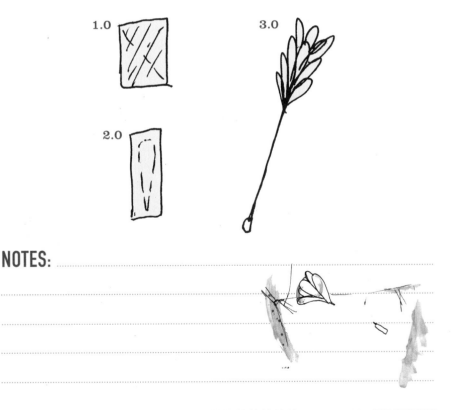

1.0

2.0

3.0

NOTES:

Gia keeps her dog close, keeps her in line, keeps her from jumping on old ladies and shows other dog owners that a pup can be pimped out without a rhinestone leash.

MATERIALS

- DT (black, pink)
- Leash clasp

1.0 Make about a 55" leash: Work with 1 arm's length of black tape at a time. LSB, SSS each piece along the V-axis. Attach pieces together by sandwiching overlapping ends. Do not fold over the last strip.

2.0 Before you fold over the last strip, SSB and SSU, cut along the V-axis from the bottom about 2" up. Flip up the LFT flap, SSS. Then flip it over to the RT, E2E.

2.1 Fold over the rest of the strip as in Step 1 then loop the sticky tab through the leash clasp to attach.

3.0 Repeat Steps 1.0-2.1 with pink tape.

4.0 Begin from the clasp and twist the pink and black tape around each other. Once you reach the end, make a loop (for a handle) and wrap DT around the ends.

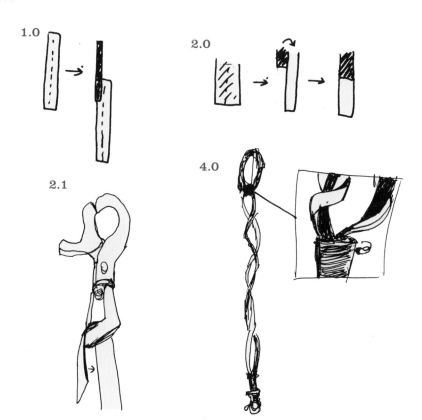

1.0

2.0

2.1

4.0

6.10 **✳✳✳✳**

CHILLAX

Six o'clock. Friday. When Ryan tells his dad he's borrowing the car to take Linda on a date, he throws him these flip-flops and the TV remote and runs.

MATERIALS
- DT (gray)
- Cardboard

TOOLS
- Utility knife

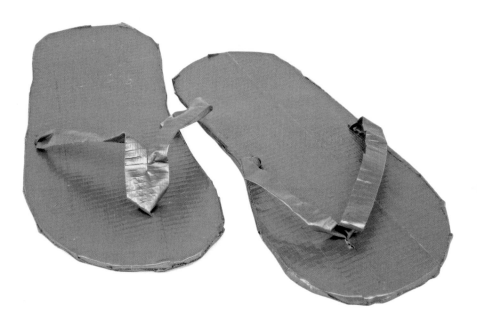

- Option #1: Trace a pair of flip-flops you own onto the cardboard.
- Option #2: Place your foot on the cardboard and trace around it.

1.0 Cut out the cardboard flip-flop bottoms.

2.0 Cover the tops and sides in DT.

3.0 To create flip-flop straps: Cut two 10" strips and fold SSB, SSS, E2E along the V-axis.

3.1 Leave one 2" margin at the top of each and cut along the V-axis to that point.

To attach the straps to the cardboard:

4.0 Option #1: Place your foot on top of the flip-flop and make one ¾" mark between the big toe and the second toe and two more slits about ¼" from each side of the middle of the flip-flop.

Option #2: Use a regular flip-flop as a guide to where the straps should go.

4.1 Feed the 2" margin into the slot between your toes and the other 2 ends through the remaining slots. Insert your foot between the straps and adjust the tightness by pulling the straps from the bottom. Then remove your foot carefully—trim the strap ends and tape them to the bottom.

5.0 To complete the flip-flops, adhere tape to each bottom and trim the edges.

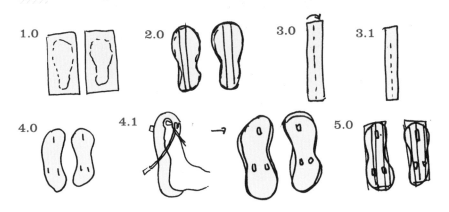

1.0   2.0   3.0   3.1

4.0   4.1   5.0

✳ ✳ ✳ ✳
PUSHER

Adelaine acts with her attitude all the time. She doesn't care what people think or say about her. Just don't push her buttons, especially not these ones.

MATERIALS

- DT (red, yellow, blue)
- Sheet of cardstock (or junk mail postcards)

TOOLS

- Circle template (half-dollar coin or a one-inch button)
- Hole punch (⅛")

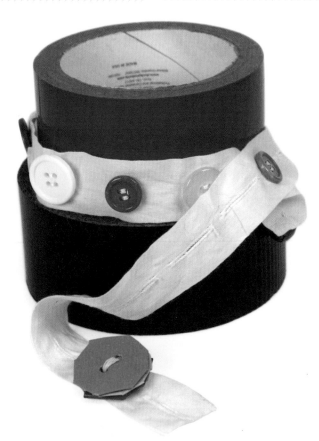

1.0 Use a round object like a half-dollar coin or a one-inch button and trace the shape a few times onto the sheet of cardstock.

2.0 Cut out the circles.

3.0 Use one 2" strip of DT to cover each circle. Place the circle in the middle of the DT piece and make slices before folding, as seen in the illustration, to avoid buckling tape.

4.0 Punch two holes into each button. Layer buttons and colors and sew onto fabric for decoration.

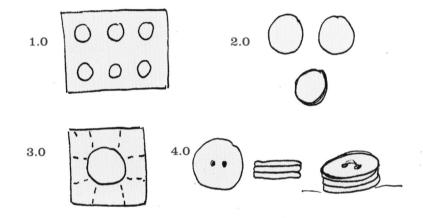

1.0   2.0   3.0   4.0

NOTES:

SURVIVOR

Tommy constantly tripped up in life. He blamed it on his shoelaces and lack of loyalty to his friends. He no longer blames it on his laces.

MATERIALS

• DT (black, yellow)

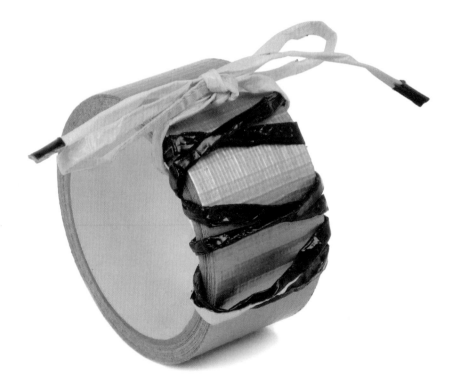

1.0 Cut one 18" strip of yellow and black tape.

2.0 Tape each strip individually, SSB, SSU, and cut from the lower RT corner diagonally to the upper LFT corner.

3.0 LSB, SSU, lay out the triangles as follows to create 2 rectangles that connect (allow edges to overlap): black, yellow, yellow, black.

4.0 Cut across the H-axis. Save both strips.

5.0 SSU, roll 1 strip from the top to the bottom.

5.1 Attach that piece so one end overlaps the end of the unrolled strip and proceed to roll the second strip.

6.0 Trim the laces to your desired length, then tightly wrap 1 small black strip around each end.

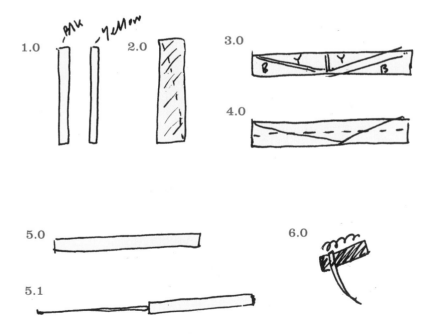

TORN

Cora used to cry when the kids would steal her headband. Her teacher thought it was because kids were mean. But really, Cora just hated how her hair looked without her headband.

MATERIALS

- DT (any color)
- Braided elastic

- Option #1: Use a headband you own as an example.
- Option #2: Measure around the crown of your head with a string/tape measure.

1.0 Cut elastic to the length you determined. Then cut 1 DT strip a little shorter than that measurement.

2.0 DT LSB, SSU, place the elastic along the H-axis, with the ends hanging over each side, and fold the DT over SSS top to bottom, E2E.

3.0 With the elastic along the top edge, cut zigzag, jagged slices along the bottom edge.

4.0 Knot together the two ends of the elastic to complete.

1.0

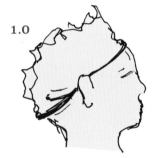

2.0

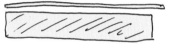

3.0

4.0

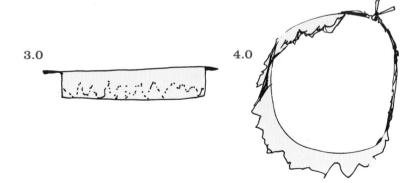

✳✳✳✳

LADY

As a child, Marcy danced in her mother's doorway, like she was at the Moulin Rouge. As an adult, Marcy decorates her hair with this barrette and still likes to pretend—it makes her feel pretty.

MATERIALS

- DT (red, white, yellow)
- 2" auto barrette

1.0 SSU, cut a "V" into each red strip. The bottom of the "V" should be a little over ¼" and should slant to about the half way point.

1.1 Fold the top edge over ⅛". Then fold the strip into thirds, bringing the LFT and RT sides SSS. Repeat this process proportionately for the white pieces.

2.0 At the end of each "petal," create fringe by slicing 3-4 times longwise.

3.0 Adhere the petals to the barrette in a compass pattern—first lay down the red ones in North, South, East, and West positions, then the white on top of the red in Northeast, Southeast, Southwest, Northwest positions.

4.0 Finally cut one ½" yellow circle and adhere it to the middle of the white petals.

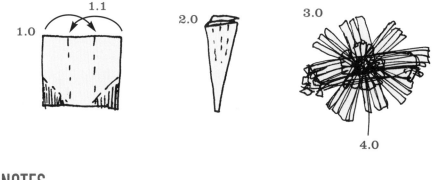

NOTES:

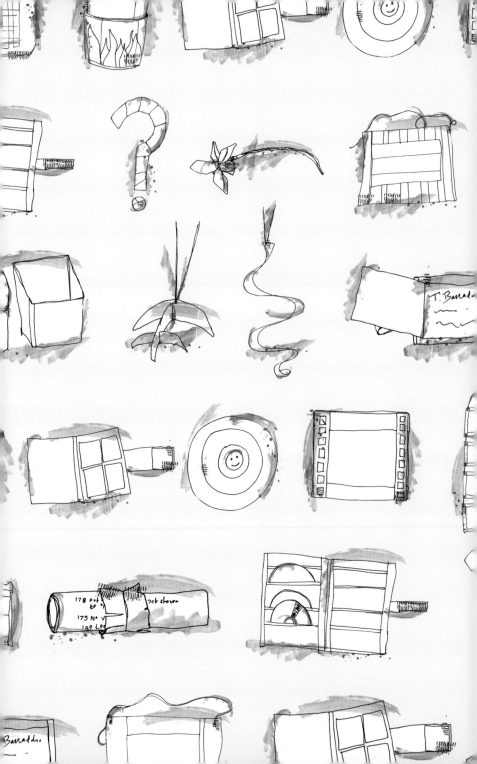

CHAPTER SEVEN

GOODS & DÉCOR

SILENCIO

A gentle wind blows across Matthew's face as he calmly stares out his kitchen window towards the city, and down to his placemat full of country photos, where he wishes he could be.

MATERIALS

- DT (brown, grass-green, orange, yellow)
- Clear packing tape
- Cardstock/photo (8½" x 11")

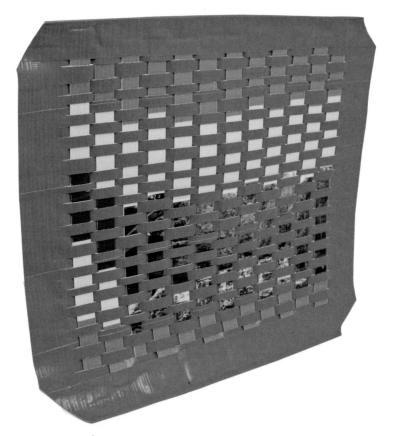

1.0 Create 1 green sheet 9" x 11". LSB.

2.0 Keep 1" margins around the perimeter and make horizontal slices within that border that will create varying warp thicknesses (¼"- ½").

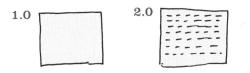

FOR WEFT:

1.0 Print or adhere a photo of nature onto one 8½" x 11" sheet of thick paper. "Laminate" the photo with clear tape. If there is white space left around your image, add colored DT (such as yellow, orange, or brown) to fill that space.

1.1 LSB, slice vertically every ½" until the whole sheet is cut up. (Note: You will only need 12 strips to weave.)

FOR WEAVING THE PLACEMAT:

1.0 Begin with Weft 1 and bring it up from the bottom of Slit 1. Then push it down through Slit 2. Repeat that pattern until it reaches the end. With Weft 2, push it through the top of Slit 1 and pull it up through Slit 2. Repeat the pattern until the weave is complete.

2.0 To seal the weft in place, wrap one 11" green strip over each side. Trim edges.

3.0 Cut off the placemat corners at a diagonal.

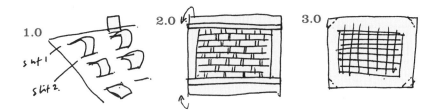

7.1 ✳✳✳✳
SCORCHER

It's 8:30AM. Work at 9:00AM. Five minutes to snooze. Five minutes to dress. Ten minute coffee-prep. Remember coffee sleeve. Ten minute commute. Faith and Finnigan like it hot when they grab-n-go with their coffee.

MATERIALS

- DT (dark-blue, red, orange, yellow)
- Cardboard "hot drink" sleeve

1.0 Rip apart cardboard sleeve and cover it front and back with vertical strips of blue DT. Trim edges as necessary.

1.1 Reform into a ring—slightly overlap the ends and wrap 1 strip of DT around them to seal it.

2.0 Lay out 1 strip of yellow, orange, and red DT onto your cutting mat. Slice flame-shape variations into each one.

3.0 Adhere "flames" over the blue background. Experiment with layering different colors/shapes.

1.0

1.1

2.0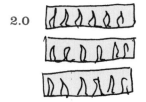

3.0

NOTES:

CONNECT

Cassie was so crazy about her phone that she carried it with her wherever she went. So did everyone else she knew. So she made this phone case to always remember which one was hers.

- DT (any color)
- Soft fabric
- Velcro

1.0

Measure the approximate dimensions of your phone and cut a piece of fabric to the estimated height and three times the length of it, plus 1".

2.0

Cover the back of the fabric in DT. Leave a little extra DT at each end, cut out a square at each corner, and wrap the DT over the fabric edges to complete the sheet.

3.0

Fabric side up, fold the sheet into thirds. Leave the top flap up and the remaining flap will be sealed to create the pouch for your phone.

4.0

Seal the LFT and RT edges.

5.0

Add Velcro on the middle of the inside top flap and its corresponding closing point.

6.0

To create a little pocket on the outside of the case, make a sheet the same length as your case and desired width. Seal the outer edges to complete the case.

.

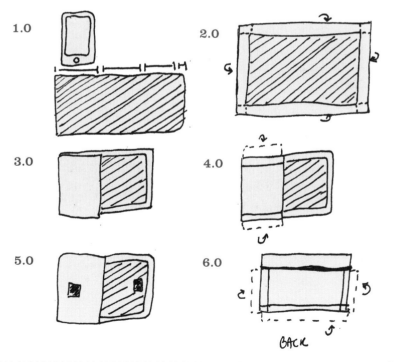

1.0

2.0

3.0

4.0

5.0

6.0

BACK

7.3 ✳✳✳✳
DIZZIES

Izzy's not sure where these trippy coasters came from, but someone made them for him. Maybe it was his sister, maybe a neighbor, or maybe (he thinks) an alien.

MATERIALS

- DT (royal-blue, orange, purple, yellow)

Create one 5" x 5" blue sheet. Cut out 1 circle with a 4" diameter.

On a cutting mat, place two 4" orange strips SSD, with their long edges overlapping. Cut out 1 circle with a 3" diameter and adhere it to the middle of the blue circle.

On cutting mat, place one 3" purple strip SSD. Cut out 1 circle with a 2" diameter and adhere it to the middle of the orange circle.

On cutting mat, place one 2" yellow strip SSD. Cut out 1 circle with a 1" diameter and adhere it to the middle of the purple circle.

With permanent marker, draw a smiley face on the yellow circle.

1.0

2.0

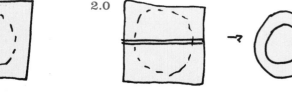

3.0

4.0

5.0

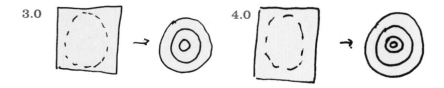

NOTES:

IDOL

"Isn't he swoony?" Sandra says as she kisses his photo in this magnetic frame and slams her locker. Her friend walks arm-to-arm with her, and rolls her eyes.

MATERIALS

- DT (gray)
- 2-circle-shaped magnets
- Clear packing tape
- Gaffers tape (black, white)
- Double-stick tape

For the back of the frame: Create one 5½" x 7" gray sheet (LSB). On the first strip SSU, place 2 magnets in the middle at least 3" apart and proceed to create the fabric as usual.

Make one 4" x 6" clear window, by layering clear tape SSS.

Sandwich each edge of the clear window between 2 strips of gray DT, to create 1 frame. Trim the DT edges to match the size of the back pieces. Then place 1 double-stick strip of tape along the underneath of the clear window.

Align the front frame on top of the back pieces and wrap strips of DT around the LFT, RT, and bottom edges to seal them together.

Decorate the front like a film frame: Add black tape all around it. Then cut small white squares out of tape and place them along the LFT and RT sides, spacing them out in a column.

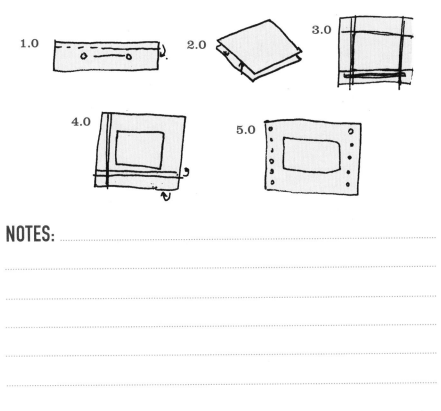

1.0   2.0   3.0

4.0   5.0

NOTES:

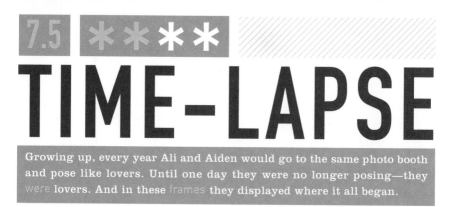

TIME-LAPSE

Growing up, every year Ali and Aiden would go to the same photo booth and pose like lovers. Until one day they were no longer posing—they were lovers. And in these frames they displayed where it all began.

MATERIALS

- DT (black)
- Wire (24-gauge, black)

TOOLS

- Long needle nose pliers
- Wire cutter

1.0 Set aside four 2" x 2" black sheets for the backs of your frames.

Cut out one 1¼" x 1¼" square from the middle of each of the other 2" x 2" black sheets. Keep the frame and discard the square.

2.0 Place each window on top of 1 whole black sheet. Line up and seal the LFT, RT, and bottom edges by wrapping one ½" strip along each side.

3.0 Punch 1 small hole in each corner and insert photos into the frames.

3.1 Line up the frames into a column and loop wire between the bottom and top holes to connect the frames together. To hang, attach 1 piece of wire to the top 2 holes of the top frame.

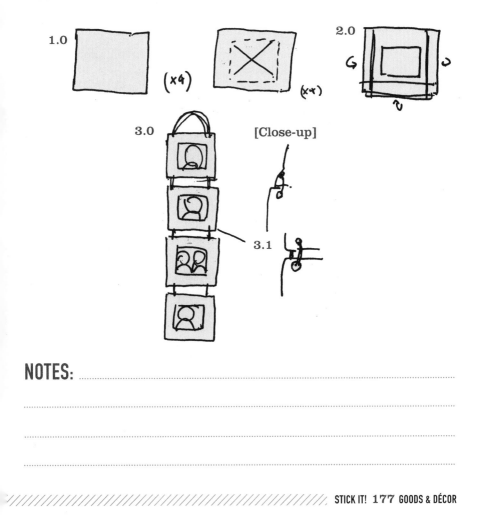

1.0 (x4)

(x4)

2.0

3.0   [Close-up]

3.1

NOTES:

MOODY

Some days Ember's on fire. She's passionate, playful, the ideal image of perseverance. But even Ember loses her spark on Mondays and plants her face in this pillow.

- DT (royal-blue, gray, white)
- Pillow stuffing (or old T-shirts, cotton balls, etc.)

Create two 10" x 10" blue sheets.

Line up the 2 squares on top of each other and seal 3 adjacent sides, by wrapping 10" blue strips over each.

Open the un-taped end and insert your pillow stuffing. Then to seal the last side, press the lips together and wrap one 10" strip around the edges.

Decoration option: Add tapes front to back and cut off the edges at the pillow seams.

1.0

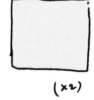

(x2)

2.0

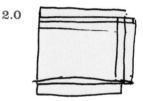

3.0

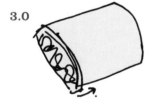

4.0

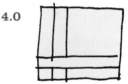

NOTES:

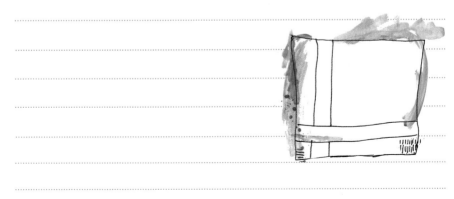

SEASONED

Briton blew everyone away with his brilliant decorations for every season. This wreath, without a doubt, was a front door feature for November . . . until it literally blew away.

MATERIALS

- DT (green, orange, red, yellow)
- Transparent nylon thread

TOOLS

- Stapler

DT COMPONENTS:

- Six 6" green strips
- Six 6" orange strips
- Six 6" red strips
- Six 6" yellow strips
- Six 7" green strips
- Six 7" orange strips
- Six 7" red strips
- Six 7" yellow strips

1.0 Make a cross with two 6" green strips. Staple the middle.

2.0 Pull up the four ends and join them with a staple. It should resemble a sphere-shape, which will act as one wreath-link.

3.0 Repeat steps 1.0-2.0, matching the sizes and colors of the DT strips. You should end up with three wreath-links of each color and size.

4.0 Join the 6" wreath-links together end to end with the stapler, to form the inner circle of the wreath. Repeat with the 7" wreath-links to form the outer circle of the wreath.

5.0 Place the inner circle into the outer circle and staple wreath-links together to complete the wreath. Add thread to hang.

1.0

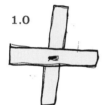

2.0

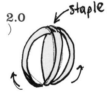
staple

3.0

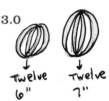

Twelve 6"   Twelve 7"

4.0

inner circle   outer circle

5.0

JAZZED

Madame Mosley had mixed emotions about hangy things in her house, but when her grandson made her this mini chandelier she couldn't resist admiring it.

MATERIALS

- Wire (18-gauge)
- DT (silver and white)
- Transparent nylon thread

TOOLS

- Small circle template (baby food jar lid)

1.0 For the base of the chandelier, make three wire rings covered in silver DT—one 25", one 20", and one 15".

2.0 Cut twenty 6" pieces of transparent thread and set them aside. These will be hanging-units off of your chandelier base.

3.0 Place strips of white DT SSD onto a cutting mat. Use a small circle template (like a baby food jar lid) to trace circles onto them and cut them out with a craft knife. You are going to need eighty circles to complete the whole chandelier, but you do not need to cut them all out at once.

4.0 To create a hanging-unit, start by sandwiching one piece of 6" thread you cut from Step 2.0 between two circles SSS at the very end of the thread.

4.1 Repeat the process about 1" up from that adhered circle.

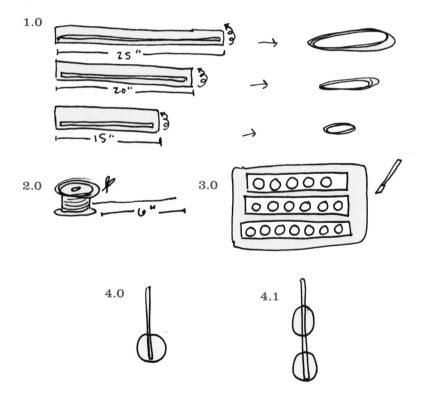

1.0

25"

20"

15"

2.0

6"

3.0

4.0

4.1

Once you have repeated steps 4.0-4.1 to complete twenty hanging units, use small pieces of silver DT to adhere and hang them to the bases of the chandelier in a clock pattern. The two big rings will have 8 hanging-units each, and the smallest ring will have 4 hanging-units.

Layer the rings inside of each other, with the smallest in the center. Then use 1" x 3" pieces of silver DT to link the ring bases together.

Add string or clear thread to the large ring base to hang.

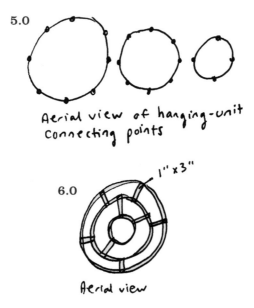

5.0

Aerial view of hanging-unit connecting points

6.0

1" x 3"

Aerial view

NOTES:

7.9 ✳✳✳✳

STRIPER

Keri could tell when a piece of furniture was past its prime. She liked it that way, because it meant she could turn it into something treasured, something true again . . . like this taped table.

MATERIALS

- DT (various colors)

1.0 Before you cover any old furniture (or cheap, new furniture) in DT, be absolutely positively sure that you will never want to return it to its original state. Once you start DT-ing, you can't go back.

2.0 Because everyone will have different furniture, here is a general tip: go into the project with a plan. Think about color combinations and patterns (patches, stripes, etc.) ahead of time.

3.0 Take your time and attempt to hide ragged DT edges for a more streamlined look.

NOTES:

＊＊＊＊

MAYBELLENE

At five years old her mother caught her stealing a fancy napkin ring to wear as a bracelet. She never punished her because she was Maybellene, forever "lovable."

- DT (red, orange)

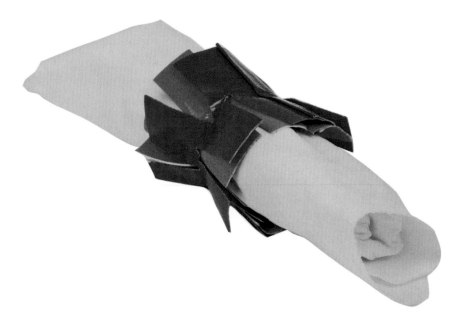

1.0 Cut one 8" red strip and one 8" orange one.

2.0 For each strip, SSB, SSU, leave one ¼" margin at the top and fold the bottom edge up to that point.

3.0 For each strip, LSB, with the tab SSU, make 1 vertical cut every ¼" to the H-axis, alternating between the bottom and the top.

4.0 Fold each band into 1 ring and seal the ends with the sticky tab. For presentation, insert 1 ring within the other for a layered effect.

1.0
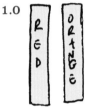

2.0
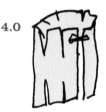

3.0

4.0

NOTES:

BAILA

The music moves Manuel and Macy, even as they eat. Their toes tap the floor. Their forks synch with the rhythm of their conversation as they flip through their music collection in this CD case.

MATERIALS

- DT (gray, red, black)
- Adhesive Velcro

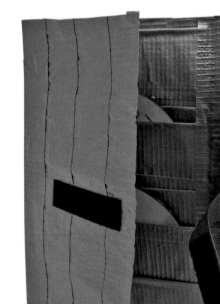

1.0 Cut one 6" red strip. SSB, fold along the V-axis SSS, E2E. This tab will be the case closure.

2.0 For CD case: create one 10" x 14" gray sheet, LSB, with vertical strips. Before you fold over the last piece to seal the edge, slice 1¼" center along the fold. Then feed the end of the red tab through it from underneath, fold the flap over and seal the end into place.

3.0 For CD pockets: Use seven 6" gray strips to create 1 sheet that's about 5½" x 6" (LSB). Fold the bottom up towards the top—let the fold occur naturally. Create 6 of these pockets.

4.0 Cut strips to seal pockets onto the case:
- Six ½" x 6"
- Two ½" x 10"
- One 1½" x 10"

4.1 Begin with the top LFT area of the case.
(a.) Judge the distance; your first pocket should be from the top by inserting 1 CD into it. Seal the bottom edge of that pocket with one ½" x 6" strip.
(b.) Below the first pocket, place another pocket and adhere one ½" x 6" strip to the bottom of that one, too. Repeat the process for the third one as well.
(c.) Repeat (a.)-(b.) on the RT side of the case.
(d.) Adhere the ½" x 10" strips vertically over the sides of the pockets on the far LFT and RT of the case.
(e.) SSD, run the 1½" x 10" strip down the middle of the case, overlapping the edges of the pockets on both sides.

5.0 Close the case and apply Velcro to the tab and front of the case.

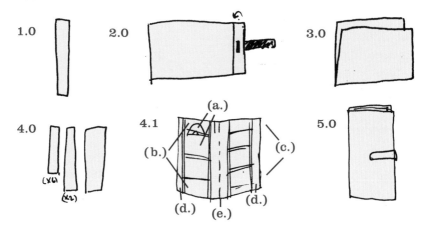

✳✳✳✳

TRANSFORMER

Everyone knows Frida as the famous Tape Artist who can transform any wall into treasured art. Her parents named her after Frida Kahlo. All she really wanted to be was Mona Lisa.

MATERIALS

- DT (various colors)

TO CREATE A WORK OF ART WITH DT:

1.0 Whether you use a sheet of paper or a wall as your canvas, start out by creating a frame out of tape to mark the space you are to work within.

2.0 Various techniques for "painting" with tape:

(a.) modern mood—large blocks of color made by bumping solid colored DT E2E to create a "mood."

(b.) impressionist's eye—very thin and short slices of DT, that when used in a large quantity can create the "impression" of various forms and colors.

(c.) bold 'n' the beautiful—utilizing silhouette structures for a bold statement.

(d.) abstract exclusion—the process of cutting out shapes, discarding the positive and keeping the tape with their negative space.

1.0 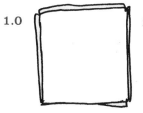 2.0 (a.) 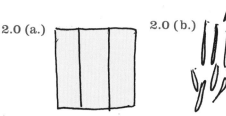 2.0 (b.)

2.0 (c.) 2.0 (d.)

NOTES:

....

....

....

....

....

....

....

INFATUATION

Rose is a firecracker. Violet is shy. But when either of them gets this flower, there's no denying why.

MATERIALS
- DT (white, grass-green, yellow)
- Wire (18-gauge)

TOOLS
- Wire cutter

To create the stem: With the green strip LSB, SSU, trim ½" horizontally off of the bottom and put to the side to use later. Then place the wire horizontally on the top edge and roll it in the DT completely.

To create a base for the petals to stick on to:
(a.) Take one 2" yellow strip and make 1 diagonal cut half way to the center, from each corner.
(b.) Place the middle of the yellow square on top of the stem and wrap the edges over and around the stem.

To create white petals (one 2" DT = 1 petal):
(a.) SSU, fold the upper LFT and RT corner to the V-axis.
(b.) Fold the LFT and RT slanted edges to meet the V-axis.
(c.) Cut the piece into a diamond-shape, but leave at least one ¼" squared edge at the bottom.

Stick the petals SSD onto the yellow base in a compass pattern: place the first 4 in North, South, East, and West positions, then place the next 4 on top of them in Northeast, Southeast, Southwest, Northwest positions.

To create the center of the flower: Cut out 1 yellow circle, big enough to cover the middle of the flower where the petals connect, and adhere on top.

With the ½" x 8" green strip, wrap it around the base under the petals to secure.

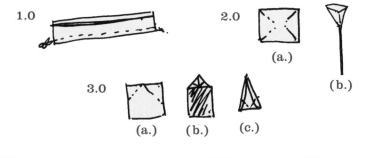

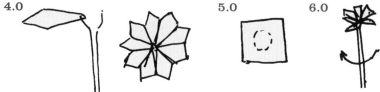

WORD

Life gets overwhelming sometimes. Steve knows all about this. Just check his changing sign. He's king of stayin' alive in the sludge he calls life.

MATERIALS
- DT (black, white)
- Artist tape (½", yellow)
- String
- Non-permanent marker

TOOLS
- Hole punch

1.0 Create one 5½" x 7" white sheet (LSB).

2.0 Cut four 7" black strips and wrap 1 around each side of the white sheet to create a frame.

3.0 Adhere yellow tape in equidistant vertical strips.

4.0 Punch 1 hole in the LFT and RT corners and attach string through them.

5.0 Apply lettering with non-permanent marker onto the white area.

Tip: Remove marker with water and a paper towel and change messages often.

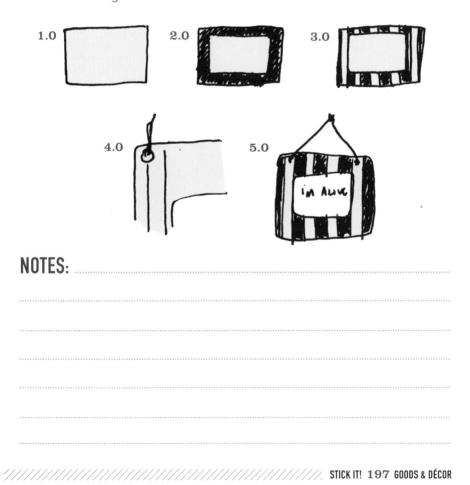

NOTES:

7.15 ✳✳✳✳

LINGER

At work, April savors the scent of a fresh spring day with her flower tacks. Minus the pollen. And the rain. And the bugs. Ah, yes, all of its beauty.

- DT (yellow)
- Round flat tack

For the center flower base:
(a.) Take 1 square SSU and fold each corner into the center point to form a smaller square.
(b.) Trim it into an even smaller square (½" x ½").

To create petals (one 2" DT = 1 petal):
(a.) SSU, fold the upper LFT and RT corner to the V-axis.
(b.) Fold the LFT and RT slanted edges to meet the V-axis.
(c.) Cut the piece into a diamond-shape, but leave at least one ¼" squared edge at the bottom.

Stick the petals SSD onto the yellow base in a compass pattern: place the first 4 in North, South, East, and West positions, then place the next 4 on top of them in Northeast, Southeast, Southwest, Northwest positions.

Pierce the round tack through the center of the flower.

1.0

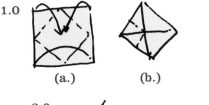

(a.) (b.)

2.0

See p. 194, steps 3.0 (a.)-(c.) ["Infatuation"]

3.0

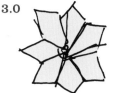

4.0

NOTES: ....

....

....

....

....

....

BLOWOFF

"Sayonara, sucker!" said sixteen-year-old Roxanne as she revved past a 1958 Cadillac. She liked to believe she was the best at everything. Until the Cadillac passed her off and left her reading this bumper sticker in the dust.

- DT (yellow)
- Adhesive vinyl letters

1.0 Cut a 10" yellow strip.

2.0 Apply lettering: BYE BYE BYE!

Tip: For alternate text variations, play with filling in the blank, " Stick It! to _____ .

1.0

2.0 BYE BYE BYE!

NOTES:

BYE BYE BYE!

UNTAMED

She woke up one morning with her curly hair looking as crazy as her keychain. Wild Thing, Wren thought as she zipped up her hoodie.

MATERIALS

- DT (black, orange, yellow)
- Steel split ring

- One 4" yellow strip
- One 3" orange strip
- One 2" black strip

1.0 SSB, SSU, leave one ½" margin at the top of each strip and fold in half from the bottom to that point.

1.1 Cut vertical fringe (about ¼" thick) along each piece.

2.0 SSD, alight the top ½" margins of each piece and layer, from the bottom to the top: yellow, orange, black.

3.0 SSU, fold the whole piece into thirds, wrapping the LFT and RT sides over the middle.

4.0 Punch 1 hole in the middle of the top and attach the steel split ring.

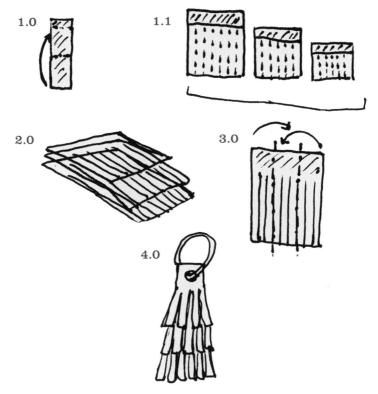

DAPPER

The clock is ticking, the pressure is on, the test is almost over, but the only thing Luke can think about is making mustache-faces at Emily with this pencil topper.

MATERIALS

- DT (black)

TOOLS

- Mustache template (see pg. 205)

1.0   Cut one 6" black strip.

2.0   LSB, SSU, fold the strip SSS along the V-axis into a rectangle.

3.0   Trace the mustache pattern (based on the template) onto the sheet and cut it out.

4.0   Make two parallel horizontal slices on the lefthand bar of the mustache. Slip the pencil top through the two slices.

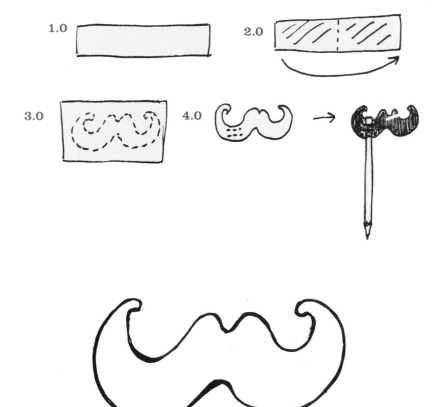

RULED

Maurice didn't like rules. Not in school. Not in games. Not in life. But he liked to make his own rules. And in this case he carried the pencils and pens to make his mark.

MATERIALS
- DT (plaid and blue)
- String

TOOLS
- Hole punch (¹/₈")

1.0 Make one 8" x 14" sheet, with patterned DT on Side 1 and a solid-colored DT on the reverse side (Side 2).

2.0 Find the center point of the RT edge and cut at an angle toward the upper LFT and lower LFT edges, to create an envelope-point.

3.0 Punch a hole in the area of the point and attach one 12" piece of string.

4.0 Using a ruler as a guide, leave a 1" margin on the LFT side and make five 1" horizontal slices about 2" from the top. Between each slice, leave a 1" space. Once you've finished that series of line slices, move your ruler down about ¼" and repeat. Repeat the same process 2" from the bottom.

Tip: Play with the spacing of your slices to accommodate the length of your writing instruments.

5.0 Weave your pencils and pens between your slices.

5.1 Roll it up.

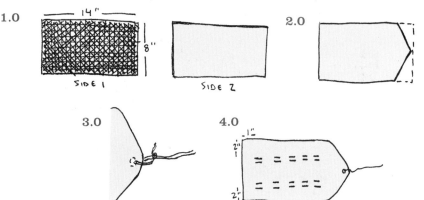

FLURRY

Beatrix turns to ice when she gets mad. When the night is frozen over, not even hot cocoa can melt her cold heart. The only thing that does is making a snowflake ornament.

MATERIALS

- DT (silver or white)
- 1 sheet of paper (8 1/2" x 11")
- String

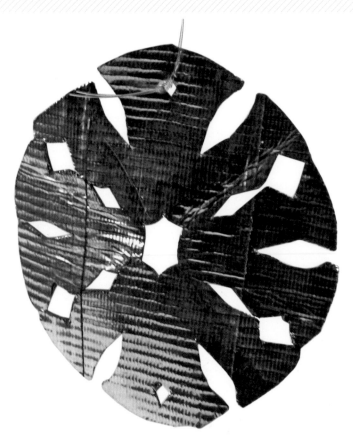

1.0 Create one 5" x 5" DT sheet. Set it aside.

2.0 Cut a paper snowflake to use as a template. Begin by cutting down the sheet of paper to 5" x 5".

2.1 Fold the sheet of paper diagonally in half to form a triangle.

2.2 Fold again diagonally to form a smaller triangle.

2.3 Fold the triangle into thirds. Shift the paper so the sides meet before you crease.

2.4 Cut horizontally across the base of the triangle to create a straight edge.

2.5 Cut into the edges of the triangle to create your snowflake pattern. Then unfold.

3.0 Place the piece of paper over your DT sheet and trace the pattern. Then remove the paper and cut out your DT snowflake. Add string to hang.

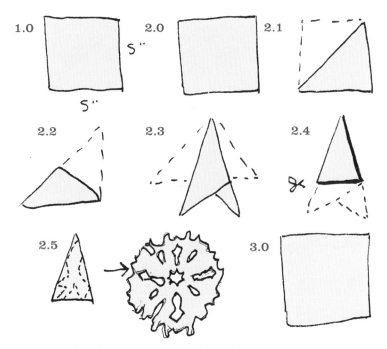

SPEEDY

Little things amuse Twyla. Little, fast things. Like twirling and spinning tops. Dizzying things. Her sister should have never made this ornament for her.

MATERIALS

- DT (gray)
- Wire (24-gauge)

TOOLS

- Wire cutter

1.0 Bend wire into the shape of a swirl, with a diameter of 6-8".

2.0 SSU, join strips of DT together (the length of the swirl). Place the wire on top and sandwich it by placing strips SSD on top of them.

3.0 You should be able to feel and see where the wire is in the DT sheet. Trim around the wire on the outer edges and discard the scraps. Then make 1 curly cut, following the shape of the swirl to the center.

4.0 Hold the outer end of the swirl and the inside should fall and whirl. Punch 1 hole in the outer end and attach the string.

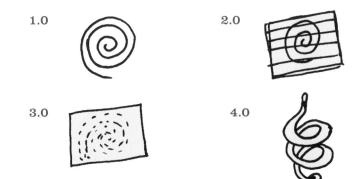

1.0

2.0

3.0

4.0

NOTES:

FREE-FALL

As he watches his luggage fall onto the conveyor belt with this tag, it reminds Az of those pool days, jumping into the deep end, sometimes flipping in air. That brief moment of freedom before crashing through water.

MATERIALS

• DT (blue, white)

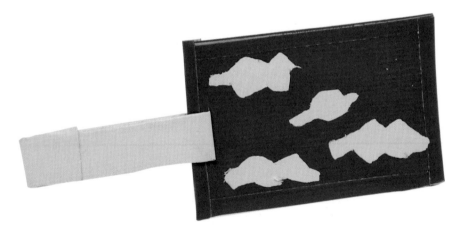

1.0 For tag: Cut two 6" blue strips. SSB, fold each along the H-axis, E2E. (1 rectangle will be the back of the tag; 1 will be the front.)

2.0 For top tag: Work with 1 rectangle LSB and keep ½" margin on the LFT side and ¼" on the other sides. Make 1 slice along the top, RT, and bottom sides parallel to the edges along the ¼" borders.

3.0 Cut: two ½" x 3" blue strips and two ½" x 2" blue strips.

3.1 Place the top tag on top of the other rectangle. Align the edges and wrap the edges with strips to seal them together.

3.2 Cut one 1" vertical slit ¼" from the LFT edge, centered, through the 2 layers.

4.0 For the tag ring: Cut 1 white 6" strip.
(a.) Take the strip, SSB and SSU, and cut along the V-axis from the bottom about ½" up.
(b.) Flip up the LFT flap, SSS. Then flip it over to the RT, E2E.
(c.) Cut down the V-axis. Use 1 band as your ring.

5.0 SSU, feed the band through the slit in the tag and seal the tab ends together.

5.1 Turn the tag over and decorate—cut out cloud-shapes from white DT and adhere to the top.

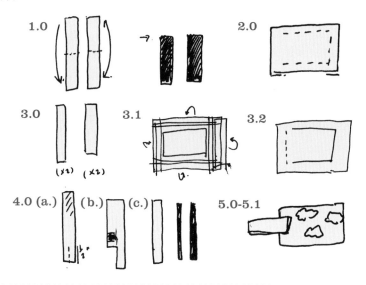

POSSESSION

There's my girl, Theo thinks as Zoe enters the party. The same thought jolts Holt and Max. And Zoe thinks of this frame in her bag no one knows is for that girl.

MATERIALS

- DT (gray)
- Adhesive vinyl letters
- String

TOOLS

- Hole punch

1.0 For the back of the frame: Create one 6" x 8" gray sheet (LSB).

2.0 Make one 4" x 6" clear window, by layering clear tape SSS.

3.0 Sandwich each edge of the clear window between 2 strips of gray DT, to create 1 frame. Trim the DT edges to match the size of the back pieces. Then place 1 double-stick strip of tape along the bottom side of the clear window.

4.0 Align the front frame on top of the back pieces and wrap strips of DT around the LFT, RT, and bottom edges to seal them together.

5.0 Punch 1 hole into the LFT and RT corners and attach string through them.

6.0 Apply lettering: MY GIRL

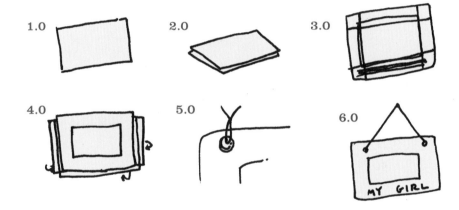

1.0   2.0   3.0

4.0   5.0   6.0

MY GIRL

NOTES:

7.24 ✳✳✳✳

TOXIC

Poison Apple Red lipstick makes Cleo a killer when she wears it out. She puckers her lips and slides it on in this mirror, then tucks it away in its holder only to reapply after she kisses her victims.

MATERIALS

- DT (red)
- 4 square mirrors (1")
- Double-stick tape
- Adhesive Velcro

1.0 With five 2½" red pieces, create one 2½" x 4½" sheet of DT fabric (SSB). Do not fold over the fifth strip—leave SSU.

2.0 Make one 1" slice along the H-axis of the SSU piece.

2.1 Cut one 2½" black strip and fold SSS longwise to 1". Then cut one ½" lime-green piece and wrap it around the end of the black tab. Feed ⅛" of the tab end through the slit, from underneath. Then fold up the bottom edge SSS to seal the fabric as usual.

3.0 Fold the red fabric in half, along the H-axis, crease, and unfold.

3.1 Adhere double-stick tape to the backs of four 1" square mirrors and place SSD on the bottom square of the fabric.

4.0 Fold the top square over the bottom square and adhere Velcro to the tab and top of the case for closure.

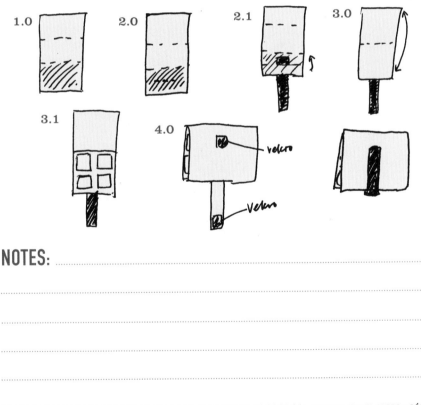

NOTES:

****

HAZE

Reading, like librarians Larry and Laura, is a trip. Through wordy lands and sentence seas, the cultural climate can cause a haze. Even they sometimes need to pause and plant this bookmark until it passes.

MATERIALS

- DT (purple, gray)

TOOLS

- Hole punch

1.0 For the bookmark body: Cut one 12" purple strip. SSB, fold SSS along the H-axis. Cut along the V-axis and punch 1 hole in the middle at the top.

2.0 For bookmark tassel, cut:
- One 3" gray strip
- One 2" gray strip

2.1 SSB, SSU, leave one ½" margin at the top of each strip and fold in half from the bottom to that point.

2.2 Cut vertical fringe (about ¼" thick) along each piece.

3.0 SSD, align the top ½" margins of each pieces and layer, from the bottom to the top, the short strip on top of the long one.

4.0 SSU, fold the whole piece into thirds, wrapping the LFT and RT sides over the middle.

5.0 Punch 1 hole in the middle of the top.

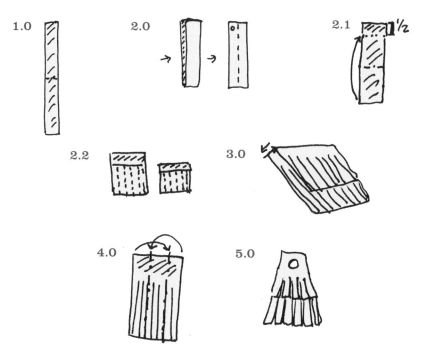

For the bookmark string: Cut one ¼" x 6" gray strip. LSB, SSU, cut 1 small vertical slice ¼" from the LFT side, still keeping it attached to the whole. Exclude that piece, and fold the bottom to the top, E2E.

Thread one end through the tassel hole and connect the other end by the sticky tab remaining to create a loop.

Loop the lead end of the tassel string through the bookmark hole and then slip the tassel through the lead end and gently tug into place.

6.0   **6.1**

7.0

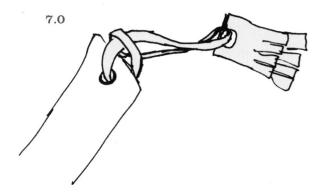

NOTES:

BREATHE

Every morning Merriam opens her eyeglass case and sets her senses racing for the day. Today she clears her mind and schedule . . . and reminds herself to just breathe.

MATERIALS

- DT (grass-green, lime-green, white)
- Padding (tissues, thin foam, etc.)

1.0 Measure approximate dimension of glasses. Add 1" to the width and height.

2.0 Create 2 grass-green sheets using those measurements. Between the first strip SSU and the second strip, sandwich your padding (such as tissues) and continue to create the fabric as usual.

2.1 Trim 1" from the height of 1 of the sheets.

3.0 Place the 2 sheets on top of each other and cut 3 strips of DT:
• Two ½" x height
• One ½" x width
Wrap each strip around the side with its coinciding measurements.

4.0 To "paint" a tree scene for the front case:
• One ¼" x 1¼" brown strip (tree trunk)
• One lime-green fluffy-shape (treetop)
• Four white DT cloud-shapes
Adhere these elements to the front of the eyeglass case. Use 1 cloud to seal the top flap.

1.0

2.0

2.1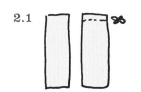

3.0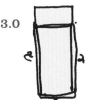

4.0

NOTES:

CHAPTER EIGHT

PAPER GOODS

8.0 ✳✳✳✳
COOLIO

Unlike all of the schoolboys, Dan's textbook cover goes beyond his mom's boring book-covering technique. He thinks he's a freak. The other kids think he's actually pretty cool now.

- DT (gray, other optional colors)

Cut 1 gray sheet using the following formula:
- Height = Height of the book + ¼"
- Width = Width of the book x 3

Sandwich the book between the big DT sheet and wrap the ends over into the front and back covers. Create the DT edges and remove the book.

Measure the width of the flaps you created and cut ½" wide strips of DT to that length. Wrap the ½" strips over the top and bottom edges of the flaps to the sheet behind it.

Decorate the cover as cool as you want with various tapes.

1.0

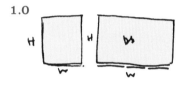

2.0

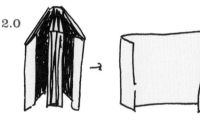

3.0

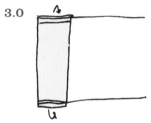

4.0

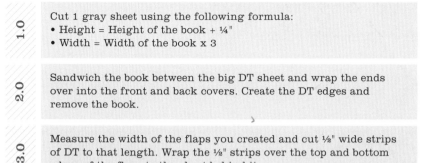

NOTES:

WANDERER

Jen's heart holds a navigation system even her brain can't understand.
And her passport cover in her pocket, her only proof of wanderlust.

MATERIALS

- DT (red)

TOOLS

- Label maker

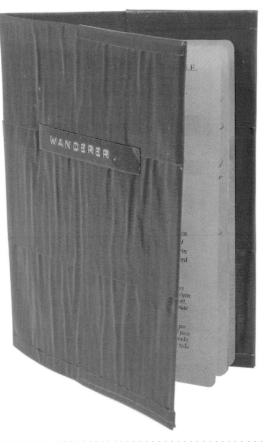

1.0	Create one 5½" x 12" sheet with DT. Keep the LSB.
2.0	To make one 2" pocket on the LFT side, fold the LFT vertical edge towards the center. Repeat on the RT side.
3.0	Cut 4 DT strips (2" x ½"). Wrap them around the top and bottom edges of the pockets to seal them into place.
4.0	Fold the whole sheet along the V-axis.
5.0	With the labeler, create lettering: wanderer. Adhere it across the front of the holder.

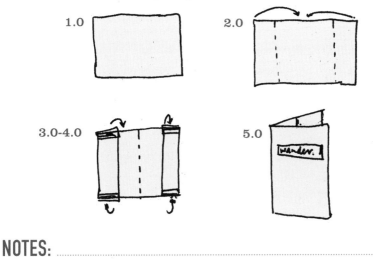

NOTES:

Luna loves the flames of fire. But the doctors ordered her to stay away from them, and they gave her this notebook instead.

MATERIALS
- DT (dark-blue, red, orange, yellow)
- 4 sheets of paper (8½" x 11")
- Waxed thread

TOOLS
- Needle

SSB, fold 4 sheets of paper together along the V-axis, E2E.

Cut in half along the H-axis, to make two 4-¼" x 5½" folios.

Insert 1 folio into the other, spine to spine, and trim the RT vertical edge slightly, back to 4¼".

To create the book cover: Make one 8¾" x 5¾" blue sheet. Then LSB, fold along the V-axis, E2E, and insert the folios, spine to spine.

To sew the folios to the cover: Work with the book open, spine horizontal, and make sure to keep the folio and cover spines in line. Poke 1 hole in the middle, along the spine, then 1½" to each side of that hole, poke another one.

Cut 1 piece of thread 3 x the height of the book. Then thread your needle and begin sewing from the inside of the book. Push your needle through the middle hole, then bring it up through the RT hole and all the way over down through the LFT hole (skip the middle hole). Then bring it up through the center hole. Straddle the 2 thread ends between the long stitch and knot them over it.

To decorate the outer spine: Cut ¼" red, yellow, and orange strips. SSU feed each strip under the spine string and SSS to create "flag flames."

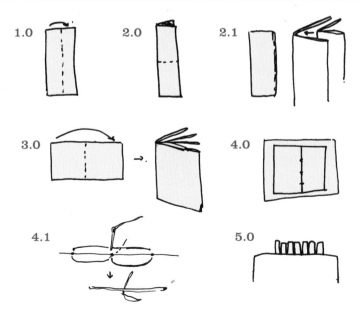

1.0   2.0   2.1

3.0   →.   4.0

4.1   5.0

GOLDEN

When Rusty found his old toy robot he believed he could hear a tick-tock within its tin wall. It oddly reminded him of a business man in a gray suit whose heart goes ca-ching as he whips out his checkbook holder.

MATERIALS

- DT (gray)
- Pro-sheen metallic tape (gold)

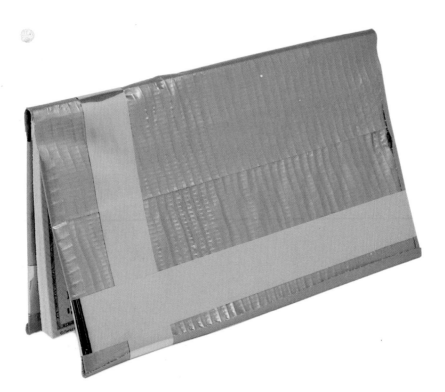

- One 6¼" x 6¾" gray sheet
- Two 6¼" x 2¾" gray sheets
- Four 2¾" x ½" gray strips
- Two 6¼" x ½" gray strips
- Three 7¼" gold strips
- Two 2¾" gold strips
- Two 6¼" gold strips

1.0 Start with the 6¼" x 6¾" sheet, SSB, and place one 6¼" x 2¾" sheet on the top and on the bottom. Align the edges and wrap ½" strips around the edges to seal. (Tape LFT and RT sides first, then top and bottom.)

2.0 Flip the whole sheet over and adhere the 7¼" gold strip vertically along the left side, then the 6¼" ones horizontally along the top and bottom sides. Wrap the ends of the tape around the edges.

3.0 Flip the whole sheet back over to the interior. Where the edges of the gold tape overlap, line up the 2¾" gold tape vertically and adhere. Then align and stick down the remaining 6¼" gold tape horizontally.

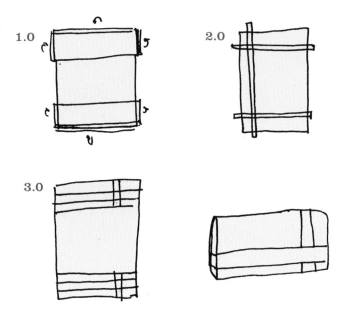

1.0

2.0

3.0

IRREPLACEABLE

She knew there had to be a reason why he wasn't calling her. Maybe he lost her card. So Elaina, in a eureka-moment, mailed him this biz card holder as a hint.

MATERIALS

- DT (white, black)
- Pro-sheen metallic tape (blue)

1.0 To create the biz card holder clasp: Cut one 2½" black strip. LSB, SSU, fold the top and bottom SSS to the H-axis.

1.1 From the bottom RT corner, cut at a diagonal to the LFT about ½".

2.0 Cut one 3¾" white strip. LSB, SSU, center one 1" horizontal slice ¼" from the top. Insert the clasp through the slice, from underneath, to about ¼" onto the sticky surface.

2.1 As if you were making a DT sheet, place one 2½" white strip SSD on top, aligning the top edge with the horizontal slice mark. Fold over the top flap.

2.2 Turn over the sheet and add another 2½" white strip SSD. SSS with the tab. ¼" from the LFT and RT edges of the newly added DT, making one ¾" slice, centered.

3.0 Cut two 4¼" blue strips and SSS them together.

3.1 Insert one end through the LFT slice, from underneath to about ¼" onto the SSU surface. Keep the blue strip underneath the SSU surface and pull the other end up through the RT slice, sticking the remaining end onto the SSU surface.

1.0

1.1

2.0-2.1

2.2

3.0

3.1

4.0

Place another 2½" white strip on top. Then continue creating a regular DT sheet with 2 more pieces.

5.0

Cut two 1½" x ½" white strips. Then fold the bottom of your card holder about ½" from the middle.

6.0

To close, fold the flap over and latch the black clasp underneath the blue strip. [Alternatively: Make a horizontal slice to the thickness of your clasp and about ¼" from the top of the blue tape—slip the clasp through the top of it.]

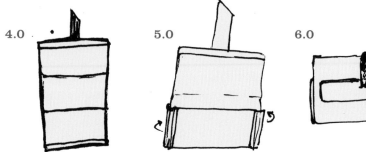

4.0   5.0   6.0

NOTES:

NOTES:

8.5 ✳✳✳✳
RUNAWAY

Whizzing through the pile of mail on the kitchen counter, Erol finds the envelope from Dee. He imagines how far it travelled across land and sea, and when he opened it, her words escape.

1.0 Create 1 sheet of white DT using this formula for envelope dimensions:
• width = height of card + ½"
• height = width of card x 2 + 1"

2.0 To seal the sides: cut 2 strips of DT (½" x width of the card). Fold the bottom edge of the envelope towards the top. Leave one 1" margin at the top and seal the LFT and RT edges by wrapping the ½" strip around them.

3.0 To seal the lip of the envelope: adhere 1 strip of double-stick tape, insert the card, and fold the lip over.

1.0   2.0   3.0

NOTES:

✳✳✳✳

LUCILLE

Lucille's friends call her a shadow dancer. She moves like melted glass, fluid and fragile, in the winter when she walks to get the mail and is surprised by this card, inspired by her.

MATERIALS

- DT (red, black)
- Sheet of cardstock (8½" x 11")

1.0	Cut cardstock in half to make two 5½" x 8½" sheets. (You will only need 1.)
2.0	With the long edge on the bottom, fold along the V-axis, E2E.
3.0	Unfold and cover the outside of the card, front and back, with long red strips. Trim edges.
4.0	Create and adhere a silhouette (based on the template—see page 264) to the front, or create your own (see page 11).

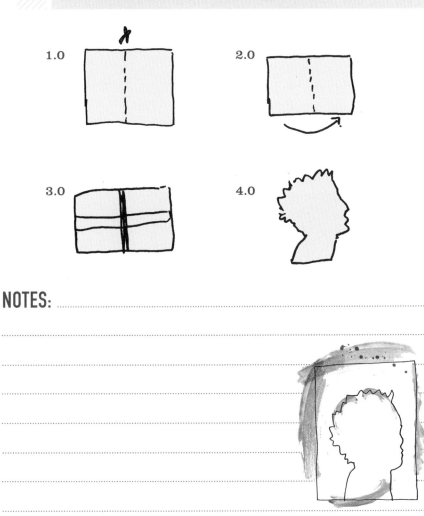

NOTES:

Page and Pam, twins from Mickabey Lane, like to drive around their small town, planning their escape. And so they sent this card to Aunt Edna, in Europe.

MATERIALS

- DT (white, royal-blue, grass-green, lime-green)
- Sheet of cardstock (8½" x 11")

1.0	Cut cardstock in half to make two 5½" x 8½" sheets. (You will only need one.)
2.0	LSB, fold along the V-axis, E2E.
3.0	Cover the front of the card with vertical blue strips until no white shows.
4.0	Create "grass": Stick one 4¼" grass-green strip and one 4¼" lime-green strip onto the cutting mat and slice triangle shapes into them.
4.1	Remove the triangles from the mat and adhere to the bottom front of the card. Repeat layering the lime-green ones over the dark-green.
5.0	Create "clouds": Stick 1 small white strip onto the cutting mat. With a permanent marker, draw clouds onto it and then cut them out.
5.1	Remove the clouds from the mat and stick them into the "sky" above the grass.

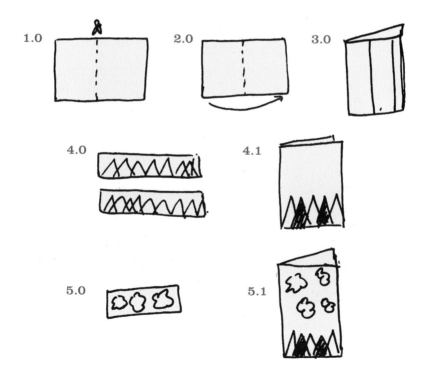

1.0 2.0 3.0

4.0 4.1

5.0 5.1

8.8 ********
RECORD

It was a serendipitous day. On the East End of town, Odele opened a card from the mail and read "My Girl." And on the West End, Octavio read "My Guy."

MATERIALS
- DT (black, white)
- Rub-on letters
- Sheet of cardstock (8½" x 11")

TOOLS
- Circle-templates (1" plastic bottle cap, masking tape)

1.0   LSB, fold the cardstock along the V-axis.

2.0   To create a card in the shape of a vinyl record: Place your large circle template on the front of the card. Allow space for the spine to stay connected and trace around the template.

2.1   Cut along the line, through both card layers.

3.0   Cover the front and back of the card using 3 long horizontal black strips. Trim around the edges.

4.0   To create a center label for the "record": Cut 1 small white strip and stick it onto the cutting mat. Trace 1 small circle template onto it, then an even smaller one within that one. Cut along those lines.

4.1   Remove the white donut-shape and place it on the center of the front of the card.

5.0   Apply lettering: [Label with whatever song title sends a message to the receiver.]

6.0   For an extra-sappy touch, cut out 1 tiny red heart and place it in the center of the record.

1.0
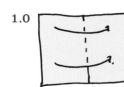

2.0

2.1

3.0
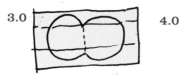

4.0

4.1

5.0   6.0

HOLIDAY

The warm glow of lights. The scent of fresh food for a family meal. A handmade greeting card in the mail. The way it all makes you, like Craig, so happy you could just pee yourself.

MATERIALS

- DT (brown, royal-blue, yellow, red, grass-green)
- Sheet of cardstock (8½" x 11")

Cut cardstock in half to make two 5½" x 8½" sheets. (You will only need one.)

SSB, fold along the H-axis, E2E.

Cover the front of the card with 3 horizontal brown strips.

Open the card up. On the back side of the brown side, measure out ⅛" margins around the perimeter and ¼" bar across both the V and H-axis. Cut out the rectangles to form a "window" once you close the card.

Create a line drawing (or silhouette-image) of a "holiday scene" on the interior white space seen through the window.

For a final "holiday" touch, close the card and create "lights" with blue, yellow, green, and red DT. Place small strips of each color SSD on a cutting mat and slice ovalish-diamond shapes. Adhere them around the brown window, alternating colors as desired.

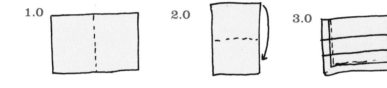

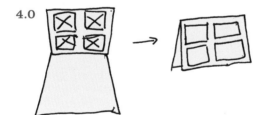

STAY

"I love you." "No you don't." "No, I hate you." "I love you." "I know. It's why I hate you." And in time Dunkin and Grace sent each other a card like this.

MATERIALS

- DT (white)
- Artist tape (½", yellow)
- Sheet of cardstock (8½" x 11")
- Rub-on letters

1.0 Cut cardstock into quarters to 4 equal 4¼" x 5½" pieces. (You will only need one.)

2.0 Cover 1 sheet front and back in white duct tape.

3.0 Cut one 5½" strip of yellow tape, and, across the card horizontally, stick along the middle.

4.0 Apply lettering: Stay (repeatedly across the yellow strip)

1.0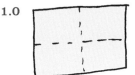

2.0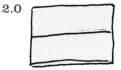

3.0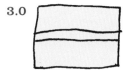

4.0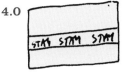

NOTES:

BABYLICIOUS

As the oldest of twelve kids, Gianna was over goo-goo-ga-gas. So when her parents announced a thirteenth "gem" to the family, she gagged. And gave them this card, with love.

MATERIALS
- DT (brown, pink)
- Artist tape (½" baby blue, yellow)
- Star deco fastener
- Sheet of cardstock (8½" x 11")

TOOLS
- Hole punch (⅛")
- Star punch

Fold the cardstock, with the LSB, along the V-axis. Then cut along the H-axis. (1 card only will be needed.)

Measure up from the bottom 2¼" and draw 1 horizontal line at that point. From the lower RT corner measure 1" to the LFT and then draw 1 diagonal line up to the 2¼" line.

Open the card and cut along the lines, in addition to along the top half of the fold. Do not discard the strip of paper.

Close the card and trim off the triangle in the lower RT corner.

Cover the front of the card with brown DT.

Add blue and yellow tape and star punch horizontally along the top edge for decoration.

Open the card and apply double-stick tape to the bottom and RT edges and close again. This is the bottom of your "basinet."

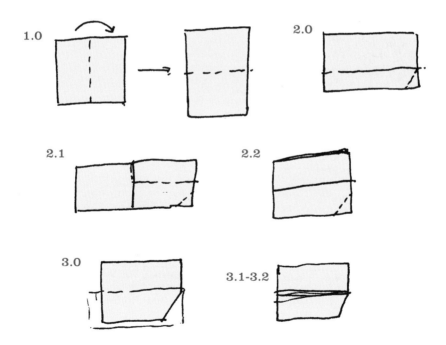

1.0

2.0

2.1

2.2

3.0

3.1-3.2

4.0	Create the "basinet hood": Cut out one 2" x 3" half circle (LSB) from the white strip of paper.
4.1	Slightly overlap the bottom of the half circle over the LFT side of the basinet (enough to be able to punch a hole in the lower LFT corner). Trace around its arc and cut along that line.
4.2	Cover the basinet hood with pink (or blue) DT and trim the edges.
4.3	Put the basinet hood back in place on top of the brown piece and punch 1 hole in the lower LFT corner. Apply star deco fastener through that hole to keep the 2 pieces together.
5.0	Apply message underneath the basinet hood.

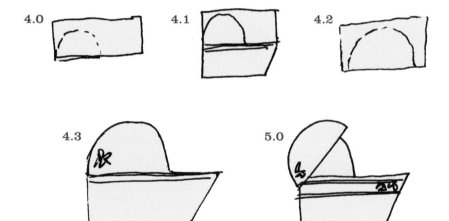

NOTES:

DIVULGE

Moms, like Joanne, say it so many times, showering it with love onto her cynical daughter. So when Joanne sends this card to her at college she can picture her rolling her eyes and saying "That's so mom."

MATERIALS

- DT (red)
- Sheet of cardstock (8½" x 11")
- Double-stick tape (½")

Fold the cardstock, with the LSB, along the V-axis. Then cut along the H-axis.

Cover the front of the card with red DT.

Tip: Ignore initial precision and overshoot the measure-ments of your strips. At the end, trim around the edges.

Open the card, the red DT face up. Keep one 1" margin on the LFT and ½" margins on the top and RT. Then slice one 1" x 4" flap from the top and one heart-shape below it in the middle of the card.

Turn over the card. Adhere double-stick tape along the interior edges and press closed.

Apply lettering with a fine-tip permanent marker:
you oughta know . . . [onto flap]
i love you. [underneath flap]

For an added decorative touch, cut out one red DT heart-shape and stick it onto the back of the card.

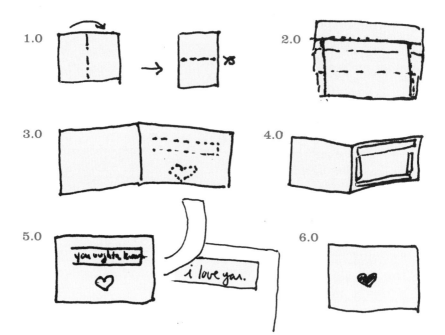

ADDICTED

"My world's a mess without you," Skylar thought. And so was his penmanship. But that didn't stop him from sending this card to Jordan.

MATERIALS

- DT (white and red)
- Sheet of cardstock (8½" x 11")

Cut cardstock in half to make two 5½" x 8½" sheets. (You will only need one.)

LSB, fold along the V-axis, E2E.

Apply lettering:
my world's a mess without you.

peace.	lonely.
love.	distressed.
happiness.	sad.

Cut 6 very thin strips (about ⅛") of red DT. Make 3 "X"s with them and adhere 1 over each word in the left column.

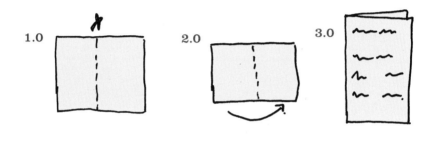

1.0 2.0 3.0

4.0

NOTES:

PRECISION

With Ashley and Spencer, actions spoke louder than words. Much louder.
That's why when it came time to say "I love you," Ashley knew this card
was the only way.

MATERIALS

- DT (white)
- White gel pen
- Black cardstock (8½" x 11")

1.0 Cut cardstock in half to make two 5½" x 8½" sheets. (You will only need one.)

2.0 SSB, fold along the H-axis, E2E.

3.0 Stick one 5½" strip of white DT horizontally across the middle of the front of the card.

4.0 Apply lettering:
i love you. [Write with fine-tip permanent marker on DT.]
i love you. [Write repeatedly in white gel pen, on the black space.]

1.0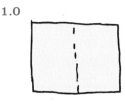

2.0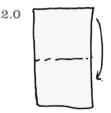

3.0

4.0

NOTES:

REVEL

Multicolored streamers and party mixes are Jon's vices. He can ruin a dude's day with his smile. Don't encourage him by giving him this card.

MATERIALS
- DT (red, yellow, blue, grass-green)
- Paper fasteners (10mm)
- Rub-on letters
- 2-Sheets of cardstock (8½" x 11")

TOOLS
- Hole puncher (⅛")

Cut 2 sheets of cardstock into quarters to equal eight 4¼" x 5½" pieces.

Cover 7 sheets front and back with DT so no white shows—2 red, 2 green, 2 yellow, 1 blue.

Create "flags" by cutting 1 triangle (3" x 4" x 4") out of each page.

Tip: Cut the eighth sheet of cardstock into that triangle shape and use it as a template—place it on top of each of the other sheets and trace around it with a fine-tip permanent marker.

Line up the cut-out flags with the 3" edge at the top, in the following order: red, green, yellow, blue, red, green, yellow. Punch 1 hole in their upper RT and LFT corners. (Do not punch 1 hole in the LFT corner of the first red flag, nor 1 in the RT corner of the last yellow flag.)

Flip every other flag upside down. Then overlap the holes of each flag, RT corners over left ones.

Apply lettering while the flags are "open"—1 word per flag:
You are the life of every party!

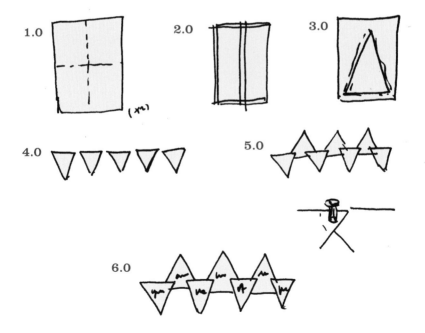

1.0   2.0   3.0   (x*)

4.0   5.0

6.0

ACKNOWLEDGEMENTS

My gratitude goes out to so many people, who like a strong, sticky strip of DT have kept me together through this book project:

Mom, Dad & V—for loving, supporting, and encouraging my "making stuff" from day one.

CH—for handing me the duct tape "seed."

JA—for saying "yes," allowing me the opportunity, and trusting my creative ways.

KC—for being the DIY book cheerleader from day one, offering encouragement and brilliance and believing in me enough to "figure it all out."

RH—for his mad design skillz that made this book look all that.

The RP fam. (esp. LC, JL, RH & FSPC)—for the support that helped me avoid DTing myself to my desk.

E, A, M, D & H—for the laughs and listening to DT daily-ish updates . . . and still being my friends.

JB, GK, EAJ, KR, HV, KM, EJ, G & EL—for being such creative, inspirational individuals in my life.

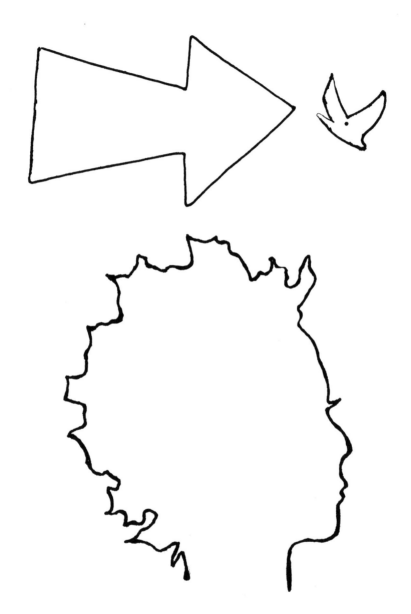